Principles
in Practice

The Principles in Practice imprint offers teachers concrete illustrations of effective classroom practices based in NCTE research briefs and policy statements. Each book discusses the research on a specific topic, links the research to an NCTE brief or policy statement, and then demonstrates how those principles come alive in practice: by showcasing actual classroom practices that demonstrate the policies in action; by talking about research in practical, teacher-friendly language; and by offering teachers possibilities for rethinking their own practices in light of the ideas presented in the books. Books within the imprint are grouped in strands, each strand focused on a significant topic of interest.

Adolescent Literacy Strand

Adolescent Literacy at Risk? The Impact of Standa

Adolescents and Digital Literacies: Learning Alongside Our Students (2010) Sara Kajder

Adolescent Literacy and the Teaching of Reading: Lessons for Teachers of Literature (2010) Deborah Appleman

Rethinking the "Adolescent" in Adolescent Literacy (2017) Sophia Tatiana Sarigianides, Robert Petrone, and Mark A. Lewis

Writing in Today's Classrooms Strand

Writing in the Dialogical Classroom: Students and Teachers Responding to the Texts of Their Lives (2011) Bob Fecho

Becoming Writers in the Elementary Classroom: Visions and Decisions (2011) Katie Van Sluys

Writing Instruction in the Culturally Relevant Classroom (2011) Maisha T. Winn and Latrise P. Johnson

Literacy Assessment Strand

Our Better Judgment: Teacher Leadership for Writing Assessment (2012) Chris W. Gallagher and Eric D. Turley

Beyond Standardized Truth: Improving Teaching and Learning through Inquiry-Based Reading Assessment (2012) Scott Filkins

Reading Assessment: Artful Teachers, Successful Students (2013) Diane Stephens, editor

Literacies of the Disciplines Strand

Entering the Conversations: Practicing Literacy in the Disciplines (2014) Patricia Lambert Stock, Trace Schillinger, and Andrew Stock

Real-World Literacies: Disciplinary Teaching in the High School Classroom (2014) Heather Lattimer

Doing and Making Authentic Literacies (2014) Linda Denstaedt, Laura Jane Roop, and Stephen Best

Reading in Today's Classrooms Strand

Connected Reading: Teaching Adolescent Readers in a Digital World (2015) Kristen Hawley Turner and Troy Hicks

Digital Reading: What's Essential in Grades 3–8 (2015) William L. Bass II and Franki Sibberson

Teaching Reading with YA Literature: Complex Texts, Complex Lives (2016) Jennifer Buehler

Teaching English Language Learners Strand

Beyond "Teaching to the Test": Rethinking Accountability and Assessment for English Language Learners (2017) Betsy Gilliland and Shannon Pella

Community Literacies en Confianza: *Learning from Bilingual After-School Programs* (2017) Steven Alvarez

Understanding Language: Supporting ELL Students in Responsive ELA Classrooms (2017) Melinda McBee Orzulak

Writing across Culture and Language: Inclusive Strategies for Working with ELL Writers in the ELA Classroom (2017) Christina Ortmeier-Hooper

Rethinking the "Adolescent" in Adolescent Literacy

Sophia Tatiana Sarigianides
Westfield State University

Robert Petrone
Montana State University

Mark A. Lewis
Loyola University Maryland

National Council of Teachers of English
1111 W. Kenyon Road, Urbana, Illinois 61801-1096

NCTE Editorial Board: Steven Bickmore, Catherine Compton-Lilly, Deborah Dean, Bruce McComiskey, Jennifer Ochoa, Duane Roen, Anne Elrod Whitney, Vivian Yenika-Agbaw, Kurt Austin, Chair, ex officio, Emily Kirkpatrick, ex officio

Staff Editor: Bonny Graham
Imprint Editor: Cathy Fleischer
Interior Design: Victoria Pohlmann
Cover Design: Pat Mayer
Cover Images: Robert Petrone and Thompson-McClellan

NCTE Stock Number: 41137; eStock Number: 41144
ISBN 978-0-8141-4113-7; eISBN 978-0-8141-4114-4

Library of Congress Cataloging-in-Publication Data

Names: Sarigianides, Sophia Tatiana, 1968- author. | Petrone, Robert, 1974- author. | Lewis, Mark A., 1973- author.
Title: Rethinking the "adolescent" in adolescent literacy / Sophia Tatiana Sarigianides, Robert Petrone, Mark A. Lewis.
Description: Urbana, Illinois : National Council of Teachers of English, 2017. | Series: Principles in practice | Includes bibliographical references and index.
Identifiers: LCCN 2017032338 (print) | LCCN 2017047588 (ebook) | ISBN 9780814141144 | ISBN 9780814141137 (pbk.)
Subjects: LCSH: Reading (Secondary)—United States. | Language arts (Secondary)—United States. | Teenagers—United States.
Classification: LCC LB1632 (ebook) | LCC LB1632 .S355 2017 (print) | DDC 418/.40712—dc23
LC record available at https://lccn.loc.gov/2017032338

Contents

Acknowledgments

This project began more than a decade ago, so we have many people to thank for their support. To begin, we would not have a project at all were it not for Nancy Lesko's seminal book analyzing adolescence. When we read her book as middle and high school English teachers, it hit us hard, implicating us in its critique and thereby requiring us to think deeply about how our own teaching of youth and preparation of English teachers needed to be reconsidered from its foundation.

We also wish to thank the many groups of teacher candidates and teachers from New York, Nebraska, Montana, Colorado, Maryland, and beyond who were the first to listen to, challenge, and try out our ideas that revising conceptions of adolescence mattered in general, but especially mattered in English teaching and in the reading of young adult literature. As seemingly solitary teacher educators trying these ideas out on our own, we would never have known that our idea had wings without your insightful responses to it.

We must also express our gratitude to the academics in the audience at our professional conferences who nodded their heads in agreement—and who pushed back against our suggestions—that reconsidering conceptions of youth could not be ignored in the teaching of English. Specifically, we wish to thank Julie and David Gorlewski, as editors of *English Journal*, who agreed that a special issue on the role of adolescence was in order after they heard our 2013 American Educational Research Association (AERA) presentation. In addition, we are so grateful for all of the incredible educators who submitted manuscripts for that special issue. Each submission helped push our thinking about what reconceptualizing adolescence could mean for our field. We also want to thank the group of scholars attending our presentation on these ideas at the Conference on English Education (CEE) in Fort Collins, Colorado, in 2013. You cannot know how encouraging it was to get a chance to respond to questions we had thought about for so many years.

There are also some colleagues—and now friends—in the field whose own work on adolescence and English teaching inspired us in ours. Carlin Borsheim-Black, Amanda Haertling Thein, and Mark Sulzer, reading and talking about your projects made our own work stronger. Thank you for teaching us about these ideas all along the way. We also want to thank Steve Bickmore and Crag Hill, who have been great champions of the Youth Lens. The three of us also wish to thank several classroom teachers who got inspired by our ideas enough to try them out in their own classes and to tell us about the ways it impacted the youth it was intended to reach. Nicola Martin, Cassidy Brooks, and Adrianna Caton, your bold efforts to translate your learning into creative, enticing lessons and projects for young people will help many more teachers get these ideas into the hands of middle and high school students.

For all three of us, one of the most supportive emails we received on this journey was from Cathy Fleischer, soon after the 2015 special issue in *English Journal* came out, telling us how much she loved and appreciated the issue. Little did we know that this response would lead to an invitation to write for this imprint. Cathy, no first-time book authors could have asked for a more patient, responsive, encouraging editor. You and Kurt Austin made this project a very fortunate adventure. Thank you.

Finally, we would each like to thank those closest to us, those whose love and support have made all of this possible: James, Alexandros, and Phaedon Stillwaggon; Kaitlyn Baron; Veronica Petrone; Matt Helm; Melissa Horner; and Walt and Janet Lewis. We would not have gotten here without you. So much love and gratitude to all of you.

Adolescent Literacy
An NCTE Policy Research Brief

Causes for Concern

It is easy to summon the language of crisis in discussing adolescent literacy. After all, a recent study of writing instruction reveals that 40 percent of high school seniors never or rarely write a paper of three or more pages, and although 4th and 8th graders showed some improvement in writing between 1998 and 2002, the scores of 12th graders showed no significant change. Less than half of the 2005 ACT-tested high school graduates demonstrated readiness for college-level reading, and the 2005 National Assessment of Educational Progress (NAEP) reading scores for 12th graders showed a decrease from 80 percent at the *proficient* level in 1992 to 73 percent in 2005.

Recent NAEP results also reveal a persistent achievement gap between the reading and writing scores of whites and students of color in 8th and 12th grades. Furthermore, both whites and students of color scored lower in reading in 2005 as compared with 1992, and both male and female students also scored lower in 2005.[1]

The challenges associated with adolescent literacy extend beyond secondary school to both college and elementary school. Many elementary school teachers worry about the 4th-grade slump in reading abilities. Furthermore, preliminary analysis of reading instruction in the elementary school suggests that an emphasis on processes of how to read can crowd out attention to reading for ideas, information, and concepts—the very skills adolescents need to succeed in secondary school. In the other direction, college instructors claim that students arrive in their classes ill-prepared to take up the literacy tasks of higher education, and employers lament the inadequate literacy skills of young workers. In our increasingly "flat" world, the U.S. share of the global college-educated workforce has fallen from 30 percent to 14 percent in recent decades as young workers in developing nations demonstrate employer-satisfying proficiency in literacy.[2]

In this context, many individuals and groups, including elected officials, governmental entities, foundations, and media outlets—some with little knowledge of the field—have stepped forward to shape policies that impact literacy instruction. Notably, the U.S. Congress is currently discussing new Striving Readers legislation (Bills S958 and HR2289) designed to improve the literacy skills of middle and high school students. Test scores and other numbers do not convey the full complexity of literacy even though they are effective in eliciting a feeling of crisis. Accordingly, a useful alternative would be for teachers and other informed professionals to take an interest in policy that shapes literacy instruction. This document provides research-based information to support that interest.

Common Myths about Adolescent Literacy

Myth: Literacy refers only to reading.

Reality: Literacy encompasses reading, writing, and a variety of social and intellectual practices that call upon the voice as well as the eye and hand. It also extends to new media—including nondigitized multimedia, digitized multimedia, and hypertext or hypermedia.[3]

Adolescent Literacy

Myth: Students learn everything about reading and writing in elementary school.

Reality: Some people see the processes of learning to read and write as similar to learning to ride a bicycle, as a set of skills that do not need further development once they have been achieved. Actually literacy learning is an ongoing and nonhierarchical process. Unlike math where one principle builds on another, literacy learning is recursive and requires continuing development and practice.[4]

Myth: Literacy instruction is the responsibility of English teachers alone.

Reality: Each academic content area poses its own literacy challenges in terms of vocabulary, concepts, and topics. Accordingly, adolescents in secondary school classes need explicit instruction in the literacies of each discipline as well as the actual content of the course so that they can become successful readers and writers in all subject areas.[5]

Myth: Academics are all that matter in literacy learning.

Reality: Research shows that out-of-school literacies play a very important role in literacy learning, and teachers can draw on these skills to foster learning in school. Adolescents rely on literacy in their identity development, using reading and writing to define themselves as persons. The discourses of specific disciplines and social/cultural contexts created by school classrooms shape the literacy learning of adolescents, especially when these discourses are different and conflicting.[6]

Myth: Students who struggle with one literacy will have difficulty with all literacies.

Reality: Even casual observation shows that students who struggle with reading a physics text may be excellent readers of poetry; the student who has difficulty with word problems in math may be very comfortable with historical narratives. More important, many of the literacies of adolescents are largely invisible in the classroom. Research on reading and writing beyond the classroom shows that students often have literacy skills that are not made evident in the classroom unless teachers make special efforts to include them.[7]

Myth: School writing is essentially an assessment tool that enables students to show what they have learned.

Reality: While it is true that writing is often central to assessment of what students have learned in school, it is also a means by which students learn and develop. Research shows that informal writing to learn can help increase student learning of content material, and it can even improve the summative writing in which students show what they have learned.[8]

Understanding Adolescent Literacy

Overview: Dimensions of Adolescent Literacy

In adolescence, students simultaneously begin to develop important literacy resources and experience unique literacy challenges. By fourth grade many students have learned a number of the basic processes of reading and writing; however, they still need to master literacy practices unique to different levels, disciplines, texts, and situations. As adolescents experience the shift to content-area learning, they need help from teachers to develop the confidence and skills necessary for specialized academic literacies.

Adolescents also begin to develop new literacy resources and participate in multiple discourse communities in and out of school. Frequently students' extracurricular literacy proficiencies are not valued in school. Literacy's link to community and identity means that it can be a site of resistance for adolescents. When students are not recognized for bringing valuable, multiple-literacy practices to school, they can become resistant to school-based literacy.[9]

1. Shifting Literacy Demands

The move from elementary to secondary school entails many changes including fundamental ones in the nature of literacy requirements. For adolescents, school-based literacy shifts as students engage with disciplinary content and a wide variety of difficult texts and writing tasks. Elementary school usually prepares students in the processes of reading, but many adolescents do not understand the multiple dimensions of content-based literacies. Adolescents may struggle with reading in some areas and do quite well with others. They may also be challenged to write in ways that conform to new disciplinary discourses. The proliferation of high-stakes tests can complicate the literacy learning of adolescents, particularly if test preparation takes priority over content-specific literacy instruction across the disciplines.[10]

Research says . . .

- Adolescents are less likely to struggle when subject area teachers make the reading and writing approaches in a given content area clear and visible.
- Writing prompts in which students reflect on their current understandings, questions, and learning processes help to improve content-area learning.[11]
- Effective teachers model how they access specific content-area texts.
- Learning the literacies of a given discipline can help adolescents negotiate multiple, complex discourses and recognize that texts can mean different things in different contexts.
- Efficacious teaching of cross-disciplinary literacies has a social justice dimension as well as an intellectual one.[12]

2. Multiple and Social Literacies

Adolescent literacy is social, drawing from various discourse communities in and out of school. Adolescents already have access to many different discourses including those of ethnic, online, and popular culture communities. They regularly use literacies for social and political purposes as they create meanings and participate in shaping their immediate environments.[13]

Teachers often devalue, ignore, or censor adolescents' extracurricular literacies, assuming that these literacies are morally suspect, raise controversial issues, or distract adolescents from more important work. This means that some adolescents' literacy abilities remain largely invisible in the classroom.[14]

Adolescent Literacy

Research says . . .

- The literacies adolescents bring to school are valuable resources, but they should not be reduced to stereotypical assumptions about predictable responses from specific populations of students.
- Adolescents are successful when they understand that texts are written in social settings and for social purposes.
- Adolescents need bridges between everyday literacy practices and classroom communities, including online, non-book-based communities.
- Effective teachers understand the importance of adolescents finding enjoyable texts and don't always try to shift students to "better" books.[15]

3. Importance of Motivation

Motivation can determine whether adolescents engage with or disengage from literacy learning. If they are not engaged, adolescents with strong literacy skills may choose not to read or write. The number of students who are not engaged with or motivated by school learning grows at every grade level, reaching epidemic proportions in high school. At the secondary level, students need to build confidence to meet new literacy challenges because confident readers are more likely to be engaged. Engagement is encouraged through meaningful connections.[16]

Research says . . .

Engaged adolescents demonstrate internal motivation, self-efficacy, and a desire for mastery. Providing student choice and responsive classroom environments with connections to "real life" experiences helps adolescents build confidence and stay engaged.[17]

A. Student Choice

- Self-selection and variety engage students by enabling ownership in literacy activities.
- In adolescence, book selection options increase dramatically, and successful readers need to learn to choose texts they enjoy. If they can't identify pleasurable books, adolescents often lose interest in reading.
- Allowing student choice in writing tasks and genres can improve motivation. At the same time, writing choice must be balanced with a recognition that adolescents also need to learn the literacy practices that will support academic success.
- Choice should be meaningful. Reading materials should be appropriate and should speak to adolescents' diverse interests and varying abilities.
- Student-chosen tasks must be supported with appropriate instructional support or scaffolding.[18]

B. Responsive Classroom Environments

- Caring, responsive classroom environments enable students to take ownership of literacy activities and can counteract negative emotions that lead to lack of motivation.
- Instruction should center around learners. Active, inquiry-based activities engage reluctant academic readers and writers. Inquiry-based writing connects writing practices with real-world experiences and tasks.

- Experiences with task-mastery enable increased self-efficacy, which leads to continued engagement.
- Demystifying academic literacy helps adolescents stay engaged.
- Using technology is one way to provide learner-centered, relevant activities. For example, many students who use computers to write show more engagement and motivation and produce longer and better papers.
- Sustained experiences with diverse texts in a variety of genres that offer multiple perspectives on life experiences can enhance motivation, particularly if texts include electronic and visual media.[19]

4. Value of Multicultural Perspectives

Monocultural approaches to teaching can cause or increase the achievement gap and adolescents' disengagement with literacy. Students should see value in their own cultures and the cultures of others in their classrooms. Students who do not find representations of their own cultures in texts are likely to lose interest in school-based literacies. Similarly, they should see their home languages as having value. Those whose home language is devalued in the classroom will usually find school less engaging.

Research says . . .

Multicultural literacy is seeing, thinking, reading, writing, listening, and discussing in ways that critically confront and bridge social, cultural, and personal differences. It goes beyond a "tourist" view of cultures and encourages engagement with cultural issues in all literature, in all classrooms, and in the world.[20]

A. Multicultural Literacy across All Classrooms

- Multicultural education does not by itself foster cultural inclusiveness because it can sometimes reinforce stereotypical perceptions that need to be addressed critically.
- Multicultural literacy is not just a way of reading "ethnic" texts or discussing issues of "diversity," but rather is a holistic way of *being* that fosters social responsibility and extends well beyond English/language arts classrooms.
- Teachers need to acknowledge that we all have cultural frameworks within which we operate, and everyone—teachers and students alike—needs to consider how these frameworks can be challenged or changed to benefit all peoples.[21]
- Teacher knowledge of social science, pedagogical, and subject-matter content knowledge about diversity will foster adolescents' learning.
- Successful literacy development among English language learners depends on and fosters collaborative multicultural relationships among researchers, teachers, parents, and students.
- Integration of technology will enhance multicultural literacy.
- Confronting issues of race and ethnicity within classrooms and in the larger community will enhance student learning and engagement.[22]

Adolescent Literacy

B. Goals of Multicultural Literacy

- Students will view knowledge from diverse ethnic and cultural perspectives, and use knowledge to guide action that will create a humane and just world.
- Teachers will help students understand the whiteness studies principle that white is a race so they can develop a critical perspective on racial thinking by people of all skin colors.
- Multicultural literacy will serve as a means to move between cultures and communities and develop transnational understandings and collaboration.
- Ideally, students will master basic literacies *and* become multiculturally literate citizens who foster a democratic multicultural society.[23]

Research-Based Recommendations for Effective Adolescent Literacy Instruction

For teachers . . .

Research on the practices of highly effective adolescent literacy teachers reveals a number of common qualities. Teachers who have received recognition for their classroom work, who are typically identified as outstanding by their peers and supervisors, and whose students consistently do well on high-stakes tests share a number of qualities. These qualities, in order of importance, include the following:

1. teaching with approaches that foster critical thinking, questioning, student decision-making, and independent learning;
2. addressing the diverse needs of adolescents whose literacy abilities vary considerably;
3. possessing personal characteristics such as caring about students, being creative and collaborative, and loving to read and write;
4. developing a solid knowledge about and commitment to literacy instruction;
5. using significant quality and quantity of literacy activities including hands-on, scaffolding, mini-lessons, discussions, group work, student choice, ample feedback, and multiple forms of expression;
6. participating in ongoing professional development;
7. developing quality relationships with students; and
8. managing the classroom effectively.[24]

For school programs . . .

Research on successful school programs for adolescent literacy reveals fifteen features that contribute to student achievement:

1. direct and explicit instruction;
2. effective instructional principles embedded in content;
3. motivation and self-directed learning;
4. text-based collaborative learning;

5. strategic tutoring;

6. diverse texts;

7. intensive writing;

8. technology;

9. ongoing formative assessment of students;

10. extended time for literacy;

11. long-term and continuous professional development, especially that provided by literacy coaches;

12. ongoing summative assessment of students and programs;

13. interdisciplinary teacher teams;

14. informed administrative and teacher leadership; and

15. comprehensive and coordinated literacy program.[25]

For policymakers . . .

A national survey produced action steps for policymakers interested in fostering adolescent literacy. These include:

1. align the high school curriculum with postsecondary expectations so that students are well prepared for college;

2. focus state standards on the essentials for college and work readiness;

3. shape high school courses to conform with state standards;

4. establish core course requirements for high school graduation;

5. emphasize higher-level reading skills across the high school curriculum;

6. make sure students attain the skills necessary for effective writing;

7. ensure that students learn science process and inquiry skills; and

8. monitor and share information about student progress.[26]

This report is produced by NCTE's James R. Squire Office of Policy Research, directed by Anne Ruggles Gere, with assistance from Laura Aull, Hannah Dickinson, Melinda McBee Orzulak, and Ebony Elizabeth Thomas, all students in the Joint PhD Program in English and Education at the University of Michigan.

Notes

1. ACT. (2006). *Aligning postsecondary expectations and high school practice: The gap defined: Policy implications of the ACT national curriculum survey results 2005–2006.* Iowa City, IA. Retrieved on July 3, 2007, from http://www.act.org/path/policy/pdf/NationalCurriculum Survey2006.pdf

Applebee, A., & Langer, J. (2006). *The state of writing instruction in America's schools: What existing data tell us.* Center on English Learning and Achievement. Retrieved on July 3, 2007, from http://cela.albany.edu

Adolescent Literacy

National Center for Education Statistics. (2002). *National Assessment of Educational Progress (NAEP). NAEP Writing–Average writing scale score results, grades 4, 8, and 12: 1998 and 2002.* Retrieved on July 3, 2007, from http://nces.ed.gov/nationsreportcard/writing/results2002/natscalescore.asp

National Center for Education Statistics. (2006). *National Assessment of Educational Progress (NAEP). Reading Results: Executive Summary for Grades 4 and 8.* Retrieved on July 3, 2007, from http://nces.ed.gov/nationsreportcard/reading/

2. Altwerger, B., Arya, P., Jin, L., Jordan, N. L., et al. (2004). When research and mandates collide: The challenges and dilemmas of teacher education in the era of NCLB. *English Education, 36,* 119–133.

National Center on Education and the Economy. (2007). *Tough choices or tough times: The report of the New Commission on the Skills of the American Workforce.* San Francisco, CA: Jossey-Bass.

3. Brandt, D. (2001). *Literacy in American lives.* New York: Cambridge University Press.

Gee, J. (2007). *Social linguistics and literacies: Ideology in discourses.* London: Taylor & Francis.

4. Franzak, J. K. (2006). *Zoom.* A review of the literature on marginalized adolescent readers, literacy theory, and policy implications. *Review of Educational Research, 76*(2), 209–248.

5. Sturtevant, E., & Linek, W. (2003). The instructional beliefs and decisions of middle and secondary teachers who successfully blend literacy and content. *Reading Research & Instruction, 43,* 74–90.

6. Guzzetti, B., & Gamboa, M. (2004). 'Zines for social justice: Adolescent girls writing on their own. *Reading Research Quarterly, 39,* 408–437.

Langer, J. (2001). Beating the odds: Teaching middle and high school students to read and write well. *American Educational Research Journal, 38*(4), 837–880.

Nielsen, L. (2006). Playing for real: Texts and the performance of identity. In D. Alvermann, K. Hinchman, D. Moore, S. Phelps, & D. Waff (Eds.), *Reconceptualizing the literacies in adolescents' lives* (2nd ed.) Mahwah, NJ: Lawrence Erlbaum, 5–28.

Sturtevant, E. & Linek, W. (2003).

7. Moje, E. B. (2002). Re-framing adolescent literacy research for new times: Studying youth as a resource. *Reading Research and Instruction, 41,* 211–228.

8. Boscolo, P., & Mason, L. (2001). Writing to learn, writing to transfer. In G. Jijlaarsdam, P. Tynjala, L. Mason, & K. Londa (Eds.), *Studies in writing: Vol 7. Writing as a learning tool: Integrating theory and practice.* Dordrecht, The Netherlands: Kluwer Academic Publishers, 83–104.

9. Lenters, K. (2006). Resistance, struggle, and the adolescent reader. *Journal of Adolescent and Adult Literacy, 50*(2), 136–142.

10. Moje, E. B., & Sutherland, L. M. (2003). The future of middle school literacy education. *English Education, 35*(2), 149–164.

Snow, C. E., & Biancarosa, G. (2003). *Adolescent literacy and the achievement: What do we know and where do we go from here?* New York: Carnegie Corporation. Retrieved June 23, 2007, from http://www.all4ed.org/resources/CarnegieAdolescentLiteracyReport.pdf

11. Bangert-Drowns, R. L., Hurley, M. M., & Wilkinson, B. (2004). The effects of school-based writing-to-learn interventions on academic achievement: A meta-analysis. *Review of Educational Research, 74*, 29–58.

Greenleaf, C. L., Schoenbach, R., Cziko, C., & Mueller, F. (2001). Apprenticing adolescent readers to academic literacy. *Harvard Education Review, 71*(1), 79–129.

12. Moje, E. B., Ciechanowski, K. M., Kramer, K., Ellis, L., Carrillo, R., & Collazo, T. (2004). Working toward third space in content area literacy: An examination of everyday funds of knowledge and discourse. *Reading Research Quarterly, 39*(1), 38–70.

13. Moje, E. B. (2007). Developing socially just subject-matter instruction: A review of the literature on disciplinary literacy. N. L. Parker (Ed.), *Review of research in education.* (pp. 1–44). Washington, DC: American Educational Research Association.

14. Kim, J. L. W., & Monique, L. (2004). Pleasure reading: Associations between young women's sexual attitudes and their reading of contemporary women's magazines. *Psychology of Women Quarterly, 28*(1), 48–58.

Kliewer, C., Biklen, D., & Kasa-Hendrickson, C. (2006). Who may be literate? Disability and resistance to the cultural denial of competence. *American Educational Research Journal, 43*(2), 163–192.

Moje, E. B., & Sutherland, L. M. (2003).

15. Moje, E. B. (2007).

Ross, C. S. (2001). Making choices: What readers say about choosing books for pleasure. In W. Katz (Ed.), *Reading, Books, and Librarians.* New York: Haworth Information Press.

16. Guthrie, J. T., Van Meter, P., McCann, A. D., Wigfield, A., Bennett, L., & Poundstone, C. C. (1996). Growth of literacy engagement: Changes in motivations and strategies during concept-oriented reading instruction. *Reading Research Quarterly, 31*, 306–332.

17. Guthrie, J. T. (2001). Contexts for engagement and motivation in reading. *Reading Online.* International Reading Association. Retrieved June 23, 2007, from http://www.readingonline.org/articles/handbook/guthrie/index.html

Guthrie, J. T., & Humenick, N. M. (2004). Motivating students to read: Evidence for classroom practices that increase reading motivation and achievement. In P. McCardle and V. Chhabra (Eds.), *The voice of evidence in reading research.* Baltimore, MD: Brookes, 329–354.

18. Biancarosa, G., & Snow, C. (2004). *Reading next: A vision for action and research in*

Adolescent Literacy

middle and high school literacy. Report to Carnegie Corporation of New York. Washington, DC: Alliance for Excellent Education. Retrieved June 25, 2007, from http://www.all4ed.org/publications/ReadingNext/ReadingNext.pdf

Guthrie, J. T. (2001).

Oldfather, P. (1994). *When students do not feel motivated for literacy learning: How a responsive classroom culture helps.* College Park, MD: University of Maryland, National Reading Research Center. Retrieved June 25, 2007, from http://curry.edschool.virginia.edu/go/clic/nrrc/rspon_r8.html; NCREL (2005).

19. Goldberg, A., Russell, M., & Cook, A. (2003). The effects of computers on student writing: A meta-analysis of studies from 1992 to 2002. *Journal of Technology, Learning, and Assessment, 2,* 1–51.

Greenleaf et al. (2001).

Guthrie, J. T. (2001).

Kamil, M. (2003).

Ray, K. W. (2006). Exploring inquiry as a teaching stance in the writing workshop. *Language Arts, 83*(3), 238–248.

20. Cai, M. (1998). Multiple definitions of multicultural literature: Is the debate really just "ivory tower" bickering? *New Advocate, 11*(4), 11–24.

Hade, D. (1997). Reading multiculturally. In V. Harris (Ed.), *Using multi-ethnic literature in the K–8 classroom.* Norwood: Christopher-Gordon.

Taxel, J. (1992). The politics of children's literature: Reflections on multiculturalism, political correctness, and Christopher Columbus. In V. Harris (Ed.), *Teaching multicultural literature in grades K-8.* Norwood: Christopher-Gordon.

21. Fang, Z., Fu, D., & Lamme, L. (1999). Rethinking the role of multicultural literature in literacy instruction: Problems, paradox, and possibilities. *New Advocate, 12*(3), 259–276.

Nieto, S. (2000). *Affirming diversity: The sociopolitical context of multicultural education.* New York: Longman.

Rochman, H. (1993). Beyond political correctness. In D. Fox & K. Short (Eds.), *Stories matter: The complexity of cultural authenticity in children's literature.* Urbana: NCTE.

Taxel, J. (1992).

22. Banks, J. A. (1991). Teaching multicultural literacy to teachers. *Teaching Education, 4*(1), 135–144.

Diamond, B. J., & Moore, M. A. (1995). Multicultural literacy: Mirroring the reality of the classroom. New York: Longman.

Feuerverger, G. (1994). A multicultural literacy intervention for minority language students. *Language and Education, 8*(3), 123–146.

Freedman, S. W. (1999). *Inside city schools: Investigating literacy in multicultural classrooms.* New York: Teachers College Press.

23. Banks, J. A. (2004). *Handbook of research on multicultural education*. San Francisco: Jossey-Bass.

Jay, G. S. (2005). Whiteness studies and the multicultural literature classroom. *MELUS, 30*(2), 99-121.

Luke, A., & Carpenter, M. (2003). Literacy education for a new ethics of global community. *Language Arts, 81*(1), 20.

24. Applebee, A., Langer, J., Nystrand, M., & Gamoran, A. (2003). Discussion-based approaches to developing understanding: Classroom instruction and student performance in middle and high school English. *American Educational Research Journal, 40*, 685–730.

Paris, S. R., & Block, C. C. (2007). The expertise of adolescent literacy teachers. *Journal of Adolescent & Adult Literacy, 50*(7), 582–596.

25. Biancarosa, G., & Snow C. E. (2004).

26. ACT, 2006.

This publication of the James R. Squire Office of Policy Research offers updates on research with implications for policy decisions that affect teaching and learning. Each issue addresses a different topic. Download this issue at http://www.ncte.org/about/over/positions/category/literacy/127676.htm. Read more on this topic at http://www.ncte.org/pubs/chron/highlights/127825.htm.

The Underlying Myth of Adolescence in Adolescent Literacy

Sophia Tatiana Sarigianides, Robert Petrone, and Mark A. Lewis

I n the middle of an interview Rob conducted with a white high school English language arts teacher from rural Montana, the teacher turned the conversation from the topic of the interview—curriculum and teaching—to the topic of conceptions of youth, particularly youth living in rural contexts. The teacher had moved to Montana from a major metropolitan area where she had taught for more than a decade, and she talked about how moving from the city to the "country" helped her think differently about youth and about how youth are understood within schools. She had this to say:

> There are some freshmen that drive tractors that are worth more than
> I make in a year. They're seriously responsible. Then they come to
> school and they're little freshmen—they're *ninth graders*. That doesn't
> work very well. You treat them like a man out there—he's responsible
> like a man out there—and then he comes to school and it's different.

Through her comments, this teacher lays out one of the central issues we discuss throughout this book. Most of us have been taught that adolescence is a natural category governed by the body. In other words, we have been taught to believe that adolescence is a naturally occurring stage, roughly between the ages of twelve and eighteen, and that adolescents are those who inhabit that category and, along with it, specific characteristics.

However, the realities of youth challenge this truism. These conceptions of adolescents as age- and body-dependent are not universal; in fact, they are highly dependent on context. For instance, the same youth who is "a man out there" is treated like a "ninth grader" when he comes to school, and "that doesn't work very well." He can handle responsibilities with equipment worth more than his teacher's annual salary on any given day in the field, yet when the same youth arrives to class, the school—and many adults and teachers in the school—regards this youth as a "ninth grader" with all the significations this age-based label carries: He is "little."

The contradictions embedded in this teacher's realizations about youth drive the three of us in our thinking about conceptions of adolescence in English language arts teaching. Specifically, this book is based on the idea that the way we, as white, middle-class, English language arts teachers, think about adolescence and our adolescent students greatly affects what we teach, how we teach, and even why we teach English language arts. In fact, adolescence is such an important concept in secondary education that virtually all of us who have gone through teacher education programs have been required to take courses (e.g., Adolescent Development) specifically focused on understanding our future students *as adolescents*. The ideas we learned in such courses are similar to those circulating in popular culture, as well as in our conversations with other adults and youths themselves: The category of adolescence is age-based, universal, and therefore, predictable. As a result, for many of us, the concept of adolescence shapes our thinking about secondary students in powerful ways.

As teachers who relied on stock views of adolescents to varying extent, the three of us have experienced what it is like to rethink our own conceptions of youth, to pay attention to how such shifts affect our own curricula and pedagogy as well as those of teachers with whom we work. We believe that reexamining assumptions about adolescence may have a similar impact on your teaching and thinking as well. We also hold that revising our teaching through such changes in thinking fits very well with other literacy practices and goals, and that making these changes in our thinking is a matter of social justice for the middle and high school students in our classrooms.

In our work as middle and high school English language arts teachers and now as teacher educators, the three of us have become particularly interested in how specific ideas of adolescence circulate in English teaching and in English education and the effects these ideas have on curriculum, instruction, and the experiences of secondary students and teachers. More specifically, from our independent and collective reading and research over the past decade, we've come to see that many dominant ways of understanding youth in education have negative consequences for students and teachers alike.

The purpose of this book, then, is twofold. First, we want to make visible the ways many people think about adolescence and, perhaps, help you to reconsider some of these views. Second, we want to demonstrate new possibilities for teaching middle and high school English language arts that become available upon reconsidering beliefs and expectations of adolescence and the youth described by this social category.

In the remainder of this chapter, we do four things. First, we make visible the dominant ways that many people, especially in the United States, think about adolescence. Second, we point out some of the ways these dominant—and problematic—views of adolescence circulate in our field of English language arts teaching. Third, we follow this section by sharing research that has helped us revise our thinking of adolescence by showing that adolescence was not always thought about the way we think of it today. Finally, we close this chapter by sharing how teachers and teacher educators can use a revised view of adolescence to offer new ways of teaching English language arts that will likely appeal to and energize the students in your classes.

What Are the Dominant Ways of Thinking about Youth?

In a recent *Washington Post* article, which was published in the "Health & Science" section of the paper, Arthur Allen summarizes current research on the "teenage brain." In the article titled "Risky Behavior by Teens Can Be Explained in Part by How Their Brains Change," Allen explains how brain-mapping technologies show scientists that teen brains look "slightly different" from adults' brains in the areas that are associated with reasoning and emotion. Allen argues that these differences may be responsible for risky behaviors, particularly when teens are among other teens, as well as "why teens' feelings of aggression, fear, and depression may be more intense than those of adults." Although the article does include arguments for how differences between teen and adult brains might be attributed more to experiences than age, one of the article's main conclusions is for both teens and parents to "be patient" as "science tells us that by age 24 the teenage brain has mostly morphed into an adult version."

Since the 1990s, when research comparing teen and adult brains began, the idea of the "teenage brain" has become pervasive and commonsensical in understanding and talking about secondary-age youth. It dominates as a way to authoritatively understand and explain youths' experiences and behavior. As an example, a recent episode of the popular *Dr. Drew Show* featured a prominent psychologist who explained a host of behavioral concerns tied to the problematic years of adolescence by invoking the now-familiar image of the "teenage brain," especially its prefrontal cortex. These perspectives on youth dominate covers of science-based, popular periodicals as well, like a recent *National Geographic* cover of a brain image titled "The Teenage Brain." Even prominent cartoonists take up the comical implications of these presumed ideas about youth. We can see this in the caption to a *New Yorker* cartoon that shows parents grounding their teenage son by saying to him, "go to your room until your cerebral cortex matures."

According to professionals relying on this scientific knowledge, the "teenage brain" concept is often responsible for youth being viewed in diminished ways, explaining their flaws and lack of development in relation to adults. In fact, rarely does thinking about youth and their "teenage brains" yield positive images of young people. Thinking of youth from the perspective of their brains—or similarly as "full of raging hormones"—emerges from biological and psychological domains of reasoning. From these perspectives, we can see that the main source for one dominant way of thinking about youth is fixed within the body: Teens are the way they are because of a biological reality. Though many of these ways of thinking about youth mention that society and culture influence the experience of adolescence, biological and psychological understandings typically supersede these others in popular and even academic and educational discourses.

The three of us are not in a position to refute brain-imaging data, nor are we interested in doing so. Rather, we repeat this common knowledge to point out its pervasiveness: Who refutes science tied to the teenage brain, especially in popular culture? And yet, even scientists studying teenage brains are not always unified in their own conclusions on the research. In the Allen article cited above, for example, the author admits that one of the leading researchers in the area acknowledges that differences between teen and adult brains may, in fact, be more the result of life experiences than age. The article explains:

> Paus [professor of psychology and psychiatry at the University of Toronto] has examined thousands of images of the teen and adult brains in his work, which is focused on alterations in the coating of brain cells. He sees differences between the two age groups, but he cautions they are subtle. So subtle, he says, that it can be difficult to say whether it is age or experience that causes the changes.

Other scientists even go so far as to say that the results of this research are either inconclusive or actually counter to the story of difference between teenage and adult brains. (For an interesting and quick read on this topic, you might refer to the *Huffington Post* article "The Teenage Brain: Debunking the 5 Biggest Myths" [http://www.huffingtonpost.com/david-moshman/adolescents-and-their-tee_b_858360.html]). Yet, given the authority that has been granted to medical science in the last 150 years, such knowledge about youth appears to be certain and irrefutable. And so, most of us accept these ideas about youth as axiomatic.

We argue that scientific understandings of adolescence function as only *one* of *many* potential ways of "knowing" youth and their experiences. Drawing from the popular 2009 TED Talk by author Chimamanda Ngozi Adichie, "The Danger of the Single Story," we are suggesting that scientific understandings of youth that emerge from brain-mapping technologies have become the "single story" of adolescence, so much so as to render invisible other, equally useful and valuable ways of making sense of the experiences of youth. In her talk, Adichie argues that any single story "creates stereotypes, and that the problem with stereotypes is not that they are untrue, but that they are incomplete. They make one story become the only story." One important goal of this book, then, is to offer more comprehensive understandings of youth so as to engender more expansive and equitable English language arts teaching practices.

Even as professionals who are not experts in biology or psychology, we identify enormous problems that stem from the single story of youth being a medicalized entity. There is a long history in the United States and beyond of scientific professionals connecting specific behaviors—and limitations—to particular groups based on knowledge located in the body: *all* women, or *all* black people, or *all* LGBTQ individuals are to be seen in particular, problematic ways, only to have that "scientific" knowledge later refuted as sexist, or racist, or homophobic. Already, even in the brief references we have shared in this opening, we see sufficient uncertainty even among scientists working with "hard data" to doubt all or some of the foundation on which certain knowledge tied to adolescence continues to be maintained. Yet, with regard to adolescence, the negative meanings mapped onto young people's bodies have not been refuted in mainstream discourses; in fact, they are relied upon as a rationale for the need for youths' surveillance, for adults' much-needed protection of all youth *from themselves* and their proclivities, and for managing what youth see and read in and beyond school.

The impact of social factors like class, race, events like war and trauma, geography (e.g., rural, urban, suburban), religion, family practices, and a host of other sociocultural factors are often denied relevance when it comes to young people. If some young people break from these stereotyped expectations of adolescence, these inconsistencies do not affect ideas about the entire social category; rather, these particular youth—like many of us as youth perhaps?—are considered exceptions to the rule. As one scholar affirms, "unlike other 'cultures,' adolescence is denied diversity. A homogeneity appears to drive the discourse surrounding adolescence" (Finders, 1999, p. 255).

So what are some of the dominant ways of thinking about youth that stem from biology and developmental psychology? For years, the three of us have asked current and future teachers in our classes and in schools, as well as friends, family, and other people we encounter who ask about our work, the following question: *When you hear the word* adolescence, *what comes to mind?* Though there are of course variations, and though the following list is not exhaustive, repeatedly we have heard the following responses:

- Reckless
- Impulsive
- Moody
- Rebellious
- Insecure
- Narcissistic
- In transition or still developing
- Hormonal
- Risk-taking
- Concerned about fairness
- Idealistic
- Peer-focused
- Irresponsible
- Unmotivated

What do you notice when you review this list?

We notice that though some positive traits appear (e.g., idealistic, concerned about fairness), the majority of the traits ascribed to youth are negative (e.g., insecure, narcissistic), indicate a need for adult oversight (e.g., risk-taking), or portray young people to be passively at the mercy of their bodies (e.g., wholly responsive to "hormones"). When we invite preservice and inservice teachers in our classes to develop these lists, one point we make is this: How many of these traits also describe adults that you know, perhaps even yourself? In other words, the circumstances of our lives often motivate the experiences of many of these traits. So, for example, taking on a new job might make us feel insecure too, even as adults.

We discuss these ideas much more in the chapters ahead, and point out the ways they show up in popular media, common analyses of youth in literature, and in diverse sociocultural settings. For now, though, we want to demonstrate how they also appear in writing focused on English teaching. Because of the prevalence of these problematic ways of thinking about adolescence, perhaps it should not be surprising that ideas about adolescence are sometimes woven into rationales for or explanations of key practices or ideas in our own field of English language arts teaching. It did surprise us, however, and perhaps it might surprise you too, to see where such ideas can be found and for what purposes. We detail a few of those examples below.

Links between Dominant Views of Youth and Teaching English Language Arts

In their book, *Building Literacy through Classroom Discussion*, literacy scholars Adler and Rougle (2005) explain how their decision to emphasize classroom discussion is grounded in their understandings of the needs and capacities of their students as being at a particular stage of life: middle school. They write:

> Middle school students *need* dialogue. They need to be able to talk about their learning with other students and with their teacher. This book is based on *this truth*. We'll even go so far as to say that dialogic forms of instruction are *ideally suited to this age group*. Why? Because these students are *now capable of independent thinking*; because they *are impassioned*—they have strong opinions about their social, intellectual, and political worlds; because they *pay keen attention to what their peers do and say*. They are *finding* their voices on many levels, and classroom dialogue provides a forum for them to do so. (p. 1, emphasis added)

Rather than arguing for or against the validity of the statements these scholars are making about middle school students, we wish to illuminate that their reasoning for a particular instructional approach (i.e., discussion) is grounded in ideas and assumptions about middle school students and their needs. One way to analyze such generalizing comments about a group might be to ask: Who *doesn't* need dialogue or enjoy hearing what others say? At which level of teaching *aren't* students "impassioned"? Don't we see these needs in younger students also? Adult learners? Are these traits really distinct to middle school students?

Similar arguments are seen among adolescent literacy scholars who promote the value of young adult literature. Again, we are not interested in arguing for or against the particular ideas of adolescence these scholars are pointing toward. For us, what is important is how and why they link particular ideas of youth with recommendations for curriculum and instruction. For example, in the opening of their book on young adult literature, Herz and Gallo (2005) write the following:

> YAL's value lies in its ability to connect students to the story immediately, because it deals with real problems and issues that are central to their lives. It helps teenagers in their search for understanding the complex world of today. The questions Who am I? and Where do I fit in? plague most adolescents during most of their formative years. (p. xvi)

Similar to Adler and Rougle, Herz and Gallo link particular ideas of youth (e.g., they are "plagued" by questions of identity) with specific curriculum for English language arts (e.g., YAL). In our own teaching, we like to ask college students questions we also ask ourselves: "Aren't you also asking questions of who you are and what the complex world is about? Isn't your own identity still shifting?" Labeling such common dynamics as "plaguing" when it comes to young people—and not to others experiencing similar identity shifts—only builds on and contributes to the problematic language enveloping and defining youth.

In one more example of many others we could share, we see how Smith and Wilhelm (2010) rely on familiar tropes of adolescence to guide teachers to improve their instruction of literary elements. In their book *Fresh Takes on Teaching Literary Elements*, one chapter focuses on conveying the importance of genre. The authors cite Northrop Frye's four basic narrative patterns of romance, tragedy, satire/irony, and comedy to do so. To discuss romance, the authors offer characteristics such as magic, love, uplifting, and positive themes. To move to the second pattern of tragedy, here is how they explain the genre:

> The second pattern is tragedy. Tragedies tell of challenge and failure and profound disappointment. *It is the pattern of adolescence, of disappointment, of misguided and failed quests. This pattern can be seen as a reaching toward maturity, of the struggle and failure that is necessary to growth.* Seasonally, it is autumnal. The themes of tragedies focus on the loss of innocence or of life, and on *the inevitability of decline.* (p. 161, emphasis added)

They close their discussion of genre by saying, "When we understand the genre of a text, then we will know what kind of conversational turn is being taken on the issues, and we will know what kinds of themes can be expressed" (p. 161). Though we agree with Smith and Wilhelm about the significance of using a text's genre to anticipate and analyze its reliance on or breaks from familiar themes and tropes, we want to draw attention to *how* they make this point. In addition to what these authors suggest "we will know" through their discussion of genre is an entire century's worth of built up ideas about adolescence as tragedy, as disappointment, as "misguided and failed quests," and as being associated with "the inevitability of decline."

As these examples show, understandings of adolescence are not scientifically or socioculturally neutral; neither are the understandings built into our field of teaching English language arts about adolescence and the texts youth are working to interpret and author themselves.

Though the above three examples reflect stereotyped views of youth as common knowledge woven into rationales to promote specific approaches to teaching English, in recent years, scholars in English education have engaged in research to map the effects of such ideas of youth in the real world of teaching. In our own research, for instance, we have shown how ideas of adolescence powerfully shape pre- and inservice English language arts teachers' conceptions of secondary students, possibilities for curriculum and instruction, and even figurations of their own identities as secondary English teachers. In two studies, Mark and Rob (Lewis & Petrone, 2010; Petrone & Lewis, 2012) reveal how a group of preservice teachers relied on many of the dominant ideas of adolescence in their thinking of their future students and in doing so, developed curriculum as a way to intervene. For example, many of these teachers viewed adolescence as a "time of identity formation" and a "dangerous terrain" (Lewis & Petrone, 2010, pp. 401–2); therefore, they built literature curricula that focused on helping their students connect to adolescent characters so that they could learn lessons about making "good" choices for personal growth.

By relying on these staid tropes of youth, these preservice teachers limited their range of possibilities for curricular and instructional approaches and thus reified both diminished views of youth and paternalistic and quasi-therapeutic conceptions of the school subject English. Michelle Falter (2016) built on this research to attempt to have her preservice teachers explore alternative viewpoints about youth and adolescence in order for them to more critically examine the images and representations of young people in popular culture (e.g., the comic strip *Zits*, teen magazines) and in young adult literature. She reports being mostly successful, yet some of her preservice teachers remained hesitant to rethink many of the dominant views we discussed previously.

In Sophia's research (Sarigianides, 2012), she shows how easily one preservice teacher drew from circulating ideas of adolescence as a period of "serious emotional and social hardships" to justify selecting *The Catcher in the Rye* for her unit: She believed that youth in the class who are also experiencing a scripted "middle adolescence" would identify with Holden's suffering. In another study (Sarigianides, 2014), Sophia examined how experienced inservice teachers raised concerns about potentially having their middle and high school students read Block's (1989) novella, *Weetzie Bat*, about youth who are sexual and who desire to parent and who do so successfully. Teachers expected the youth portrayed in "risk-taking" behaviors like sex and early parenting to be depicted in moralistic terms, as necessarily suffering as a result of these behaviors. Because the characters instead portrayed happiness, teachers worried that their own students would see the book as an endorsement and encouragement of behavior that likely dooms youths' real futures from any "promise of happiness."

In addition to this research, several other scholars in English education have demonstrated a range of links between conceptions of adolescence and English language arts curriculum and pedagogy. For instance, in an early study that has been influential for the three of us, Margaret Finders (1999) explains how ideas of adolescents as being "full of raging hormones" both prompted a group of preservice English language arts teachers to prioritize classroom management strategies above instructional approaches and made it difficult for them to see their secondary-age students as capable and able literacy learners. From this, Finders explains how dominant ideas of adolescence operate as "filters" whereby future English language arts teachers see certain things and disregard others.

Finally, English education scholars are also beginning to track the ways the publishing industry promotes and recirculates distinct, problematic views of youth in texts aimed specifically for a young adult audience. For example, Amanda Thein, Mark Sulzer, and Renita Schmidt (2013) analyzed two versions of Wes Moore's memoir, *The Other Wes Moore*, one marketed for adults and another revised for the young adult market. They found that there were significant differences in the narrative structure and content between the two versions. For example, the adult version asks readers to think about how complex societal and institutional forces influence people's lives, while the young adult version omits such questions in favor of cautioning the reader on how poor individual choices result in negative consequences. It became clear that the revisions made to the young adult version relied on assumptions about young people as being especially susceptible to poor decision making that might effect negative "adult" consequences. (For more on related research, see the annotated bibliography at the close of this book.)

Both for our students and for our own understandings of the ideas we may unwittingly be promoting through our teaching of English language arts, it makes great sense—and has enormous repercussions—for us to revise our thinking about adolescence and the youth subjected to its norms and expectations. In the next section, we share ideas gleaned from scholars who have helped us rethink ideas about youth, particularly the work of one scholar, Nancy Lesko, who has studied adolescence as a historical social category.

Reconsidering Dominant Ideas of Youth: Adolescence as a Sociocultural Construct

Adolescence was not always thought about the way we think of it today. The ideas that ground this book build on scholarship that shows how our dominant views of adolescence rely on ideas about youth constructed at a specific historical moment—the 1890s–1920s—in response to national worries and hopes about the enormous social changes taking place at the time, especially in the United States (Lesko, 2012). In fact, prior to this time that led to enormous shifts in thinking about adolescence, youth occupied positions of greater social responsibility, maintaining apprenticeships, even instructing other youth in classrooms.

Yet, as education scholar Lesko details, in response to massive social changes—changes like large influxes of immigrants, the invention of tremendous technological advances (e.g., the safety bicycle, the airplane), shifts from rural to urban settings, more women in the work force and the creation of organizations like the NAACP—social leaders developed great fears and worries. Their fears centered around shifts to the status quo that might jeopardize the standing of white, middle-class men and national and international prominence for the United States. These fears also led to changes that profoundly affected what was believed about and thought possible and best for youth.

In fact, according to Lesko, youth became the receptacles of hope *and* worry meant to address a national and social future of tremendous change and uncertainty. As a result, a range of experts that included G. Stanley Hall (1904), the "father" of adolescence, began recommending optimal activities and developmental timelines for actions that would best lead youth to an adulthood that would move the country and those particular youth "forward." It is important to note, though, that Hall and others had very particular ideas of which youth or which conceptions of youth were deemed as ideal—namely white, heteronormative, middle- to upper class youth. Some of the changes tied to ideas about adolescence that took place at the time—like child labor laws and a juvenile justice system that differentiated youths from adults—arguably improved youths' lived experiences. Yet, in many ways, the new thinking that emerged at the time—and that continues in our minds today—put changes in motion that debilitated and continues to demean youth from how they were once thought about, with particular negative consequences for youth not aligned with white, middle-class, heteronormative values and social positions.

Of course, experts' responses to problems always reflect the thinking that prevails at the time. And scholars like Nancy Lesko have shown that many of our existing beliefs about adolescence are built upon a foundation of racist, sexist, and classed beliefs from the turn of the prior century that have since been disproven. Yet, the ideas about adolescence that emerged from this problematic foundation remain largely static and inform ways that families, schools, medical professionals, and institutions still function today. In other words, while many of the racist, sexist, and classist ideologies that shaped original conceptions of adolescence have receded, the idea of adolescence as a naturalized stage of life they gave birth to has prevailed—and now exists as normative, as commonsensical.

Though we cannot do justice to the complex sociocultural history detailed in her book, *Act Your Age! A Cultural Construction of Adolescence*, we want to share some of the ideas gleaned from Lesko (2012) that lay the groundwork for ideas that we pick up in the chapters ahead. To start, the foundational concept of the entire book is that adolescence is a sociocultural construct (like gender or race, for example) and not an inevitable, predictable function of biology. However, as many scholars explain, constructs become so cemented as beliefs or certainties that they appear natural. So, Lesko's efforts—like those of many other scholars—involve making visible the history that led to these beliefs to help us question and challenge problematic expectations about youth in the present.

Understanding adolescence as a sociocultural construct means seeing adolescence as a historically situated category—a set of beliefs that has a specific historical provenance—more than a natural category whose expectations can be fully predicted and accounted for by the body's mechanisms. If, for example, you understand femininity as a cultural construct—that expectations handed down for centuries about what women are *supposed to* do and be like has more to do with a patriarchal history in control of describing others, especially women—then thinking of adolescence as a construct works similarly. Without knowing that adolescence has a long history of having been shaped in particular ways, by specific thinkers (e.g., G. Stanley Hall) and other powerful actors who put in motion scores of policies (e.g., strict age-based schooling), at particular times (e.g., from the 1890s through the 1920s), the ideas that we have come to expect and believe about youth appear as "truth." Scholars like Lesko help us to trace a specific history to this social category, indicating the problematic assumptions built into changes expected of youth, and especially showing us the even more problematic implications for young people that continue today as a result.

To get more specific, Lesko, in her analysis of adolescence as something that is historically situated, discusses a set of "confident characterizations" that many hold to be true about young people. These are not all the beliefs that "stick" to adolescents, but they indicate four key beliefs that recur in our minds when many of us think about this social category. Adolescents

1. can be understood by knowing their exact age;
2. focus nearly exclusively on their peers;
3. are governed by their hormones;
4. experience a slow, leisurely coming of age into adulthood (pp. 2–3).

Though we refer to these "confident characterizations" explicitly and implicitly throughout this book, we delve more deeply into them in Chapter 4 when we discuss new approaches to reading and analyzing young adult literature.

You might notice that these four beliefs characterize many of the negative traits we discussed previously, those traits generated by people when we have asked them to share what they think they know about adolescence. Importantly, such beliefs ignore differences among youth tied to race, class, culture, current events, gender, sexuality, and religious practices and disallow the kind of agency, dignity, and space for resistance reserved for adults. In addition, such beliefs perennially position youth in opposition to a distinct adulthood while judging them for their differences from the adults who occupy that category by age alone. In other words, adolescents are defined in relation to adults and mocked for their immaturity, irresponsibility, and lack of (adult) judgment. Yet, if youth take on behaviors reserved for adults and adulthood—like job-related responsibilities at the cost of formal schooling, or sexual experiences—they are judged as moving too quickly out of an expected "slow, leisurely transition" to adulthood.

In short, adolescents have a narrow tightrope of social expectations to negotiate, expectations that automatically exclude nonwhite, poor, nonheteronormative youth who cannot fit within these strict guidelines and norms. For example, while a "slow, leisurely transition to adulthood" is expected of adolescence, poor, working class youth expected to contribute to the family finances in order to have food and shelter are refused the ideals connected to this seemingly "natural" expectation. Similarly, youth who are "parentified"—that is, they are responsible for the well-being of their parents or younger siblings due to any one of myriad reasons (e.g., parents working multiple jobs, alcoholism, illness, absence), are not afforded a "proper" pathway to adulthood. Immigrant youth, too, often defy normative tropes of "coming of age" as they may be expected to function in various "adult" capacities within their home life. This idea is illuminated, too, at the very opening of this chapter when a teacher discusses how many rural youth are treated as adults on the ranch or farm but are ascribed meaning in schools connected to their grade level and age.

If all this sounds new and even a little disconcerting to you, that would make sense. While this and other research about adolescence as a cultural construct has circulated in academia for almost two decades, it has only recently begun to reach into teacher education courses and, even more recently, into middle and secondary English classrooms. For this reason, many of you reading this are likely encountering these ideas for the first time, as we did, deep into our teaching careers.

In the next section, we share some of the sites where this research has begun to touch our field of English language arts teaching in very recent scholarship, and in the ideas that we share in the upcoming chapters of this book. We hope that as readers of this book now, you will become knowledgeable about these ideas, and, if our own experiences in classrooms are any indication, your current and future students will be enormously appreciative of gaining access to this trove of information focused on who they are and are supposed to be.

How Does Reconsidering Adolescence as a Cultural Construct Matter for Teaching English Language Arts?

As demonstrated by NCTE's policy brief on adolescent literacy (reprinted on pp. ix–xix), the field of literacy education has come a long way in recent years. Specifically, scholars and educators have helped to counter many deficit perspectives of adolescent literacy by examining how adolescent literacies are multiple, diverse, social, and sophisticated. In addition, the field has pushed English teachers to conceptualize and create ways to make links between everyday adolescent literacies and school-based literacy practices (e.g., Alvermann & Hinchman, 2012; Kirkland, 2008; Morrell, 2004). The brief also reminds teachers of the typical reach of the language of "crisis" with regard to adolescent literacy, language that problematically situates youth and their literacy performances in terms of deficits.

Still, the brief's impact could be bolstered significantly by attending to one additional myth or misunderstanding with regard to adolescent literacy: commonsensical ideas tied to "the adolescent" in "adolescent literacy." Though we appreciate the ways that adolescent literacy scholarship has worked to complicate dominant views of adolescence (e.g., Alvermann, 2009), and the ways that many scholars rely on research that presumes youth to be capable literacy consumers and producers (e.g., Morrell, 2005), much more attention must be paid to our assumptions about "the adolescent" in "adolescent literacy" and teachers' "adult" roles in supporting and facilitating literacy practices with youth. In Table 1.1, we engage with some of the language and content of the brief to show some of the questions that we raise in relation to its efforts to address adolescent literacy in complex ways.

Table 1.1. A Review of NCTE's Policy Brief on Adolescent Literacy

Language from the brief	Questions raised by a sociocultural view of adolescence
"It is easy to summon the language of crisis in discussing adolescent literacy" (p. 1).	In what ways does the language of crisis embedded in discussing adolescent literacy reflect staid conceptions of adolescence as a social category?
Review of myths addressed in brief ⇨ Literacy refers only to reading. ⇨ Students learn everything about reading and writing in elementary school. ⇨ Literacy instruction is the responsibility of English teachers alone. ⇨ Academics are all that matter in literacy learning. ⇨ Students who struggle with one literacy will have difficulty with all literacies. ⇨ School writing is essentially an assessment tool that enables students to show what they have learned.	How might the very idea of "the adolescent" be a "myth" to consider within the context of "adolescent literacy"? How might such considerations advance the field of literacy education in novel ways?
"texts are written in social settings and for social purposes" (p. 3)	How might we reexamine the genre of young adult literature—a body of writing that names its readership, "young adults"—as texts "written in social settings and for social purposes"? How might students examine how texts represent adolescents/ce?
"Motivation can determine whether adolescents engage with or disengage from literacy learning" (p. 4).	In what ways might literacy curricula that focuses on critiquing and creating texts for their representations of youth motivate secondary students? How might this help to uniquely position youth as experts, increasing the likelihood of motivation for academic literacy practices?

Elsewhere, in a 2015 themed issue of *English Journal* that the three of us guest edited, literacy teachers and researchers focus on the ways rethinking adolescence can affect a rethinking of teaching the English language arts. For example, Alyssa Niccolini explores how banned and challenged books can provide a unique glimpse into how teachers' unease with certain topics can illuminate their own and their students' views of "healthy" adolescent development. In another article, Amanda Thein and Mark Sulzer demonstrate how analyzing the narrator, narratee, and implied reader in first-person narratives, which tend to dominate young adult literature, can reveal several assumptions about youth and adolescence present in the overall genre. In another, Tiffany DeJaynes and Christopher Curmi provide a counter-narrative to views of youth as disengaged and disaffected through a series of classroom moments that reveal their students as both "cosmopolitan intellectuals" and invested community members. Similarly, William Kist, Kristen Srsen, and Beatriz Fontanive Bishop share the story of students who initiated the use of Twitter as a tool to stop cyberbullying in their high school.

Aligned with the work of the educators discussed in the above journal issue, our book similarly aims to push the field to be thinking and putting into practice a range of ways to revise English language arts teaching through reimagining adolescence. One way we do so is by looking at two different classrooms in diverse contexts across two states, to offer textured views of what it might look like to engage in literacy practices grounded in a sociocultural view of adolescence to reenvision literacy instruction and learning. In looking across these classrooms—as well as an in-depth look at young adult literature and nontraditional assessments as a way to facilitate social justice through activism—this book offers future and current English teachers myriad ways to think both incrementally and holistically about how a sociocultural view of adolescence can reshape what they teach, how they teach, and why they teach English language arts.

More specifically, in Chapter 2, Sophia explains how one teacher asked her students to analyze *The Catcher in the Rye* through a Youth Lens (see Petrone, Sarigianides, & Lewis, 2014) grounded in a sociocultural view of youth and adolescence. In Chapter 3, Rob explains how a teacher developed a media literacy unit to help her students critically analyze representations of teenagers in a wide range of media texts and to create their own media texts to either critique dominant depictions of youth in the media or to offer revised renderings of youth in the media. In Chapter 4, all three of us talk about the ways young adult literature teaches its readers about youth, both problematically and productively. In the final chapter of the book, we present new ways to consider assessment by suggesting projects that engage students in advocacy or civic engagement and position them as knowledgeable advocates encouraging other youth and adults to reconsider views of adolescence. Finally, our annotated bibliography aims to guide you toward a range of resources to deepen your conceptual understanding of adolescence as well as to imagine new teaching practices for mobilizing such ideas for the classroom.

At the heart of *Rethinking the "Adolescent" in Adolescent Literacy* is a call to English language arts teachers to interrogate the very assumptions of adolescence that they may be operating from to reimagine new possibilities for engaging students with the English language arts curriculum. We wonder what might happen if more literacy teachers took up the idea of adolescence as a construct. We wonder what might happen if their students did as well. We believe that the focus of our book will tap into some of the growing momentum around ideas of adolescence already circulating in the field of literacy education to invigorate literacy teachers' motivation to revise and rethink their curricula with fresh ideas about adolescence and adolescent literacy.

Teaching Canonic High School Literature through a Youth Lens: Reading "Adolescence" in *The Catcher in the Rye*

Sophia Tatiana Sarigianides

Chapter Two

In the Classroom

"Why is Holden so frustrated? What's causing his nerves to be shot?"

The seniors in Rachel's (pseudonyms are used for her and all students named) AP English course are re-reading *The Catcher in the Rye* as a class after doing so independently over the summer. In Salinger's 1951 classic, Holden, a prep-school student, gets kicked out for poor performance. An outcast among his male peers, he spends much of the novel visiting sites around New York City thinking about his brother, Allie, who died of leukemia, and his little sister, Phoebe, whom he adores, all the while complaining about a host of issues troubling him.

Rachel wants students to think about the reasons behind Holden's many grumblings. Students did not like him on their first read of the novel. They saw him as whiny and wimpy, crying way too much, "especially for a boy." In guiding them through the text as a class, Rachel now wants the students to begin thinking more carefully about whether he might be justified in his complaints based on others' expectations of him as a stereotypical "adolescent."

The nine students in the class sit in a circle, fuchsia notebooks open to capture important ideas about the novel for their future writing about *Catcher*. Students wear variations on their charter school's uniform of white shirts and either khaki or blue pants or skirts. Wood-paneled floors and walls in the room expose ten-foot windows looking out to the parking lot and to the closest street. The room is quiet as Rachel moves to the thirty-foot whiteboard mounted to one wall. With a blue marker, she lists the students' reasons for Holden's shot nerves.

continued on next page

- kicked out of school

- worried about his parents' reaction

- fights with Stradlater

- his innocent image of Jane is destroyed

- thoughts about sex

- argues with Ackley

- interaction with Mr. Spencer

- parental pressure

- phony people

- misses Phoebe

After listing these, Rachel looks back at the class and asks, "Do these concerns or complaints point to anything in society? What aspect of society is causing Holden's nerves to be shot?"

Julio wants to study history in college. Social critique feels comfortable for him, so in responding to Rachel's question, Julio offers, "the phoniness of people in society."

Rachel nods. "Now we're getting somewhere. He thinks society and its people are phony and he can't relate to them. What is he rejecting in society by calling folks phony?"

Tom, a serious student who disliked the book because he felt that it reflected his own reality too closely, answered: "Pressure to conform. He's resisting it."

Rachel sets up her students to begin revising their initial views of this protagonist from a whiny *individual* to a young man legitimately protesting *societal pressures* to conform to narrow expectations of adolescent masculinity. By doing so, Rachel draws on fresh thinking that revises what society believes about adolescence: "typical" adolescent behavior may be more the result of adults' expectations of young people, and not how they "naturally" are. Guiding students to make this shift in perspective takes a lot of effort and scaffolding; understanding adolescence as a construct—rather than a stage with "natural" behaviors attached—and then applying this complex understanding to the interpretation of literary texts is challenging. It also brings instant analytic rigor to the curriculum, something especially apt for an AP course.

This chapter offers English language arts teachers a way to foreground ideas of adolescence through the literary study of canonic texts—especially texts frequently taught in middle and high school classes—that feature adolescent-age characters or the concept of adolescence. To do so, this chapter focuses on the way one high school English teacher applied a Youth Lens (Petrone, Sarigianides & Lewis, 2014), an approach to literary analysis that foregrounds representations of adolescence, to guide students to analyze Salinger's *The Catcher in the Rye*.

Having learned about a Youth Lens focused on young adult literature (YAL) through her graduate work, Rachel wanted to apply it to more canonic texts in her AP curriculum that featured adolescent characters. This chapter zeroes in on Rachel's curriculum, detailing some of the dialogues that allowed her to scaffold this complex approach to literary study. It also showcases some of the key texts and formative and culminating assessments that she relied on to teach and to evaluate her students' understanding of literature, adolescence, and the impact that literary representations of adolescence had on their lives.

In the next sections, I (Sophia) give some more context on Rachel's school to orient teacher readers; I take a closer look at the theory explaining a Youth Lens; and then I discuss how Rachel taught these ideas to her students through *The Catcher in the Rye*. When reviewing Rachel's exercises and assessments, keep in mind that this is but one way to approach teaching a Youth Lens and applying it to literary texts. At the end of the chapter, you will see some suggestions and prompts to jumpstart your thinking for how you might try this out in your own classroom.

School Context

Having just learned about applying ideas of adolescence as a construct to analyzing YAL in her graduate coursework with me, her white, middle-class teacher education professor, Rachel decided to revise her AP English 12 curriculum with these ideas about adolescence. As a black Jamaican teacher at a predominantly black and Latinx charter school in the Northeast, Rachel was motivated to bring shifts to her curriculum that would empower her students, all black, to see and to respond to the ways they were treated within and outside the school in their community as youth of color. The students respected and trusted Rachel with stories of how other teachers talked about youth, and about poor youth of color in particular. With this knowledge, and desiring to help her students, Rachel thought that teaching her students directly about ideas of adolescence through literature study would give them the intellectual armor to understand—and perhaps resist—some teachers' and adults' stereotyped impressions of them as youth of color. In other words, Rachel saw the value of a Youth Lens as more than just a critical literary tool to be applied in English class; she could imagine her students applying it to their lives.

At Rachel's school, students could take an AP class based on a teacher's recommendation or simply because they wanted to challenge themselves further. Having taught this group of students as tenth graders, Rachel knew them well but was also aware that their eleventh-grade English class had not prepared them enough for the rigors of an AP course. So, though the curriculum described in this chapter took place in an AP English class, the academic practices that we might expect of "AP students" did not apply. Students were bright, they trusted Rachel's guidance, but their prior academic experiences meant that setting up this course—especially the complex theoretical grounding for rethinking adolescence—would be a challenge for Rachel.

The curricular context for this focus was also unique this particular semester, and Rachel could take advantage of this novelty to motivate her students. First of all, Rachel explained how unusual these ideas about adolescence would be for an English class and for high school students. She had only just learned about them herself in her graduate program and thought that, as high school seniors, they would be very interested in learning them, too. Even in this move, Rachel positioned the students as capable, mature thinkers and learners ready for the complex content about adolescence they would be studying. Secondly, their learning would culminate in one traditional and one nontraditional assessment. Yes, they would be writing a practice AP-style essay about *The Catcher in the Rye* at the end of their unit, but they would also be presenting their ideas to a university audience of English teachers. We will say more about the opportunities for such unique assessments in English teaching in Chapter 5.

Theory: The Youth Lens

Building on the idea of adolescence as a construct, a Youth Lens takes the body of scholarship that sees adolescence as a cultural construct rather than a category of natural development and applies it to literary texts that represent young people. To understand how a Youth Lens works, let's first examine a more familiar critical lens: feminism. With a feminist critical lens, for example, readers first need to understand that gender is a cultural construct: Women do not all "naturally" act in "feminine" ways (e.g., domestic, demure). Rather, expectations for women are imposed by culture and get sedimented so well that they *seem* natural. So, if readers use a feminist lens, they watch for how gender gets depicted in texts. A typical question from a feminist perspective might be: What kinds of behaviors are assigned to girls and women, especially in relation to boys and men, in this text? So, a feminist lens examines representations of gender. Similarly, a Marxist lens explores the way class is depicted in texts, and critical race theory scrutinizes portrayals of race and racism. In the same way, a Youth Lens guides the study of how adolescence is depicted in literary texts. The central question of a Youth Lens is: How do texts represent adolescents/ce? (Teachers interested in more preparation on using critical lenses may wish to consult Deborah Appleman's 2015 *Critical Encounters in Secondary English* for definitions of key lenses, applications to literature, and classroom exercises for introducing lenses to students.)

The Youth Lens also foregrounds the ways in which such expectations predict—or prescribe—an adolescence that demeans most young people, and excludes many others (e.g., minoritized youth or young people who must work and so be excluded from the "leisurely" transition to adulthood we mentioned in Chapter 1 as one of the "confident characterizations" about teens). This body of knowledge is then applied to reading texts that feature adolescent protagonists or center on adolescence as a concept (e.g., the "adolescent" behavior of the adults in M. T. Anderson's dystopian novel, *Feed*, used to criticize a society that leaves off critical thinking in favor of consumption; see Lewis, Petrone, & Sarigianides, 2016). For teachers who have worked with critical lenses, this approach will be familiar; but even if teachers have not, picking up a Youth Lens through which to examine texts may very likely immediately increase your students' curricular buy-in—and possible future interest in other critical lenses—because the lens focuses on assumptions about who youth are and are supposed to be.

Examining representations of adolescence in texts is not new. Literary scholars focused on children's and YAL have questioned how adolescence is depicted in YAL for a good amount of time. For example, Alison Waller's entire book, *Constructing Adolescence in Fantastic Realism* (2010), wonders whether the imaginative opportunities available in fantastic realist texts—books mainly told through realist expectations except for an element of fantasy—offer young characters more agency than realistic fiction that is more bound by social norms. Ultimately, her analysis of forty years of young adult fantastic realist fiction shows that even with the liberties available through the genre of fantastic realism, "adolescence in fantastic realism remains locked into certain ways of being through discourses of age and gender which limit teenagers' agency in the fantastic and, in reality, merely proffer a kind of self-help empowerment that is neither political nor far-reaching" (142–43). In other words, not even in tales involving fantasy do young people get portrayed outside our current views of adolescents needing to follow scripted timelines and being ultimately powerless. I found this remarkable when I read Waller's study: not even in *fantasy* can adult writers permit young people to break with social expectations prescribed for them since the 1920s, homogeneously, without regard for differences in individual youth.

So, though Rob, Mark, and I did not know it when we began our work identifying and naming a Youth Lens (Petrone, Sarigianides & Lewis, 2014), literary scholars have studied representations of youth in texts for many years. For the three of us, naming this approach to examining texts as the Youth Lens brings together important analyses and lenses already circulating in the world of literary studies, but hardly known or applied in the teaching of middle and high school English. In addition, for us, situating this specific approach to analyzing texts in classrooms with youth who are "adolescents" themselves makes perfect sense and actually adds a social justice dimension to the work of studying and teaching English.

As we discuss throughout the book, existing views of adolescence are very problematic: They depict young people through deficit views as irresponsible, immature, irrational, and at sea about their identity. It is already problematic that any middle or high school teacher might see her students this way since it refuses young people the dignity—and the individuality—they deserve. But for English teachers, the stakes extend beyond this point. We circulate—and even exalt—texts that often portray young people in problematic ways and leave these portrayals unquestioned. Most teachers would not do so if the problematic conceptions were tied to gender, for example. We would employ a feminist lens to point out stereotyped representations of girls and women, especially, but even boys and men and the binaries dividing these categories. The same with race, or class: Conscientious teachers would not permit stereotyped views of people of color or poor people to be read in class without calling attention to them as stereotypes that are offensive. So, if conceptions of adolescence are problematic and yet are taken up without question in representations of youth in the texts we offer them in English class, then what opportunities are offered to youth reading such depictions to question and resist such representations within the texts and in real life? For example, if the texts we circulate—or the interpretations of them that dominate—rely on an adolescence that is criticized as inappropriately sullen, moody, irrational, or irritable, then what messages are we extending to youth who may have legitimate reasons for such moods or behaviors?

For us (Rob, Mark, and myself) and, as you will see, for Rachel, giving students the tools to engage this work themselves animates the political possibilities of English literary analysis and writing, and positions youth themselves as social activists able to change dominant ideas in the world that unfairly depict them. Next, let's look at the specifics of Rachel's curriculum to take note of how she launched a Youth Lens at her school with *The Catcher in the Rye*.

Curriculum

In this ten-week unit, students read two novels and one short story; four nonfiction readings on adolescence; and one piece of literary criticism on *Catcher*; and they watched a short clip from one film, *Tough Guise*, focused on constructions of masculinity, especially raced masculinity. To animate the texts and curricular methods used by Rachel, I focus on some key texts and exercises that Rachel built into the unit, detailing one especially potent means of scaffolding a Youth Lens by documenting a key dialogue and chart exercise she designed and led.

Capture Students' Initial Views of the Key Piece of Literature and of Adolescence

Rachel chose to have the students read the central text, *The Catcher in the Rye*, twice: first on their own to establish a baseline of interpretations and an understanding of the plot, and then together as a class while teacher and student effort was directed toward understanding a revised view of adolescence in order to build the Youth Lens. By doing this, she ensured that students had an opportunity to take note of these initial views—in writing, in a different exercise—so that they could return to them at unit's end to see evidence of any changes in their thinking.

To capture students' initial beliefs about adolescence, Rachel asked them to create a version of a body biography (Underwood, 1987) to express what they thought most people think of when they call up an image of a "typical" adolescent. She provided students with the outline of a body and asked them to add clothing and words around it to describe the youth. The clothing items added by students to depict adolescents were gendered. For girls, students drew midriff-baring shirts, and added multiple piercings on belly buttons, ears, and noses. For boys, they drew sagging pants with underpants showing, tattoos, and oversized baseball caps. Descriptive words surrounding the drawings included *crazy*, *promiscuous*, *rebellious*, *immature*, and *selfish*. Since the ideas tied to a Youth Lens involve a strong revision of what counts as "adolescence," and since utilizing a Youth Lens opens up new interpretive possibilities with literary texts, pausing to call attention to students' initial thoughts about this social category and the literature through exercises like body biographies allows their new learning to really stand out. Through this process Rachel's students began to realize the initial assumptions that they and most people around them were holding about adolescence, and these views were tough to shake for most of them. (See Sulzer & Thein's [2016] "Reconsidering the Hypothetical Adolescent in Evaluating and Teaching Young Adult Literature" for an important critique of how a teacher's questions and prompts for students can set up readers to think of youth in stereotyped ways.)

Utilize a Range of Texts to Unsettle Dominant Views of Adolescence

Unarguably, this facet of the curriculum currently proves to be the greatest challenge for middle and high school English teachers since much of the writing on adolescence as a construct is written in academic journals and scholarly books. Still, with sufficient support, many students can be guided to understand key principles of a historically traceable—rather than "natural"—view of adolescence. In Rachel's classroom, the single piece of learning that students referenced as helping them to rethink adolescence the most was the fact that people did not always think of adolescence the way we do today. Repeatedly, students identified the historical tracing of adolescence to a time when people's beliefs about adolescence differed from those of today as the most surprising, compelling, and transformative piece of learning in the unit.

For Rachel's class, some of this specific learning came from reading chapters from Nancy Lesko's book *Act Your Age! A Cultural Construction of Adolescence* (2012), guided by lectures from Rachel that explained Lesko's ideas more clearly. For example, from Lesko's text, students learned that, before the time when ideas about adolescence in this country changed—roughly the period from the 1890s to the 1920s—young people used to hold jobs as teachers and as apprentices. Only in relation to a range of big societal changes, including the adoption of standardized time, which influenced a shift to age-based schooling (rather than one-room schoolhouses grouping students of a broad age range), did ideas about what adolescence *should* be like begin to shift and get more normalized. Students were especially interested to hear that many of these new expectations of adolescence were based in racist, sexist, class-based ideas circulating at the time. For example, one of the ideas governing thinking at the time that adolescence was born as a social category was The Great Chain of Being: a racist hierarchy of living beings that placed white men at the top and nonwhite "savages" far beneath. In other words, the ideas that solidified into what adolescence *is* and *should be* are raced, as well as classed and gendered. This latter set of information greatly affected Rachel's classroom of black and Latinx students aware of the effects of race, class, and gender on their own schooling and experiences.

To complement Lesko's text, Rachel wove in other sources of information on adolescence. She had students read articles written by Margaret Finders, a researcher focused on teacher preparation but also on conducting studies in literacy classrooms. Finders's 2005 chapter, "'Gotta Be Worse': Literacy, Schooling, and Adolescent Youth Offenders," proved especially provocative. In this chapter of a book focused entirely on revising views of adolescence, Finders studies a middle school–level alternative-to-incarceration literacy classroom. Finders shows that the middle school students have a keen sense of how society sees them: As middle school–age young people with criminal records, and, sometimes, children of their own, society has already deemed them ruined youth. Yet every one of us needs social recognition. So Finders shows that the young people in this program make it their goal to be "worse" than society already believes they are as a way to gain and sustain recognition among themselves, even if they don't have wider social recognition beyond themselves. Finders's intervention with these youth is to invite students to take note of how society sees them and to show them how to talk back to these views—by writing a letter to a local paper about who they really are and the importance of their school to their growth and identities.

From this chapter, Rachel's students could see that *the idea* of what adolescents are supposed to be—and what they *cannot be* if they are still to be seen as "adolescents" within very narrow social expectations—cuts some youth off from schooling opportunities and from connections to the larger community. Beliefs about adolescence isolate and even exacerbate the suffering of youth who don't fit the norms of this social category.

Rachel complemented readings about adolescence with information from film that enhanced the unit. For example, watching a seven-minute clip from the 2002 film *Tough Guise*, students heard about the ways in which the media participates in perpetuating a narrow view of masculinity in its images, especially for men of color. This short film, which students discussed and processed through their response journals, ultimately focused on a view of gender that was not "natural" but culturally shaped. In other words, like the category of adolescence, the ways this film discussed masculinity as a "guise" or a set of performances pushed onto boys and men through media images that are then repeated by real people, reinforced the ideas Rachel was teaching about adolescence.

Bridging ideas of masculinity or gender as a construct to the notion of adolescence as a construct, students could consider that, like masculinity, perhaps society circulates only a narrow set of expectations of *youth*, too, which are then repeated by the young people who are told that this is how they *are*. These ideas also offered a way for students to see Holden as suffering as the result of dominant views of masculinity. For example, Holden did not think about sex the way that popular peers like Stradlater did—as something that "raging hormones" drive *all* young men to desire and to seek out from women, whether they care about the women or not. This difference in Holden contributed to his suffering since he was unwilling to conform to these expectations of conventional, heteronormative adolescent masculinity.

In addition to the excerpt from *Tough Guise*, students read Chbosky's young adult novel, *The Perks of Being a Wallflower*. A novel told in letters from Charlie to an unidentified recipient, *Perks* focuses on Charlie's new experiences and social struggles during ninth grade in ways that echo Holden Caulfield, while also shifting the context from an upper- to a middle-class protagonist. In Chbosky's hands, though, Charlie and characters like Patrick challenge expectations of masculinity, offering the class some variations on what they were seeing through Holden. By featuring a protagonist, Charlie, who is thoughtful and sincere about women, and Patrick as a gay adolescent male, the novel *Perks* helped to promote a growing sense of possibility for alternate views of youth, especially male youth. These alternate representations contributed to students' evolving interpretations of Holden as an adolescent male, and adolescence more generally for young men and women.

At unit's end, students presented what they learned to teachers at my university (an experience that I discuss further below and again in Chapter 5). In preparation for that workshop, Rachel suggested that we read Jamaica Kincaid's short story "Girl" and discuss it through the Youth Lens. In this very short piece of fiction, a girl is repeatedly given instructions—seemingly by an adult parent figure—on how to be a good girl in a poor, Caribbean context. Yet, interspersed amid the narrator's directions on how to iron a man's shirt and how to cook traditional dishes are warnings about why the girl is being given this tutelage: "to prevent yourself from looking like the slut I know you are so bent on becoming." In the final interviews with Rachel's students, several mentioned the reading and discussion of this text as helping to reinforce the ideas that young people are always thought of in contradictory terms: able to learn and do what is expected, *and* certain to break such social expectations of propriety. Seeing this dilemma in a text focused on a young girl complemented the other two literary texts read about young men, and it infuriated students who recognized the familiar dynamics across their lived experiences in and out of school. They saw themselves as young people who never measured up to the ideal of "adulthood" and who were perennially thought about in diminished and demeaning terms as youth.

To support students' understanding of all these texts, Rachel asked students to keep a response journal. Students had to lift several key quotes from each reading, and to summarize the meaning and its import next to each quotation. Sustaining these response journals and using them to launch class discussion allowed some of the ideas to process, and gave Rachel a starting point for clarifying misconceptions about adolescence as students worked to understand this material.

Incorporate Extensive Modeling and Practice of Applications of a Youth Lens throughout the Unit

Both the information about adolescence as a construct and the application of these ideas to interpreting literature are sources of new knowledge for students. The factual information about adolescence as a construct relies on complex understandings of how social forces can shape social categories. Using this to think about literature in ways that students have never done before will likely prove disconcerting to them. For this reason, making sure to build in lots of modeling and scaffolding throughout the unit will be key.

The most helpful source of modeling and scaffolding for applying the Youth Lens directly to *Catcher* was through a chart that Rachel designed (see Table 2.1). Since the questions on the chart were complex and new to the students, Rachel worked with the class to complete the chart first, on one topic, knowing that they would next have to do so in small groups on several other key topics. Because this assignment proved so crucial in guiding students to begin to think about adolescence as a construct and to apply these ideas to literature they were reading, I will take some time to document the dialogue in this key lesson in Rachel's class. As I will discuss, setting up this chart with the questions Rachel designed carefully guides students to see how specific topics (e.g., sex) and figures (e.g., parents) play strong roles in shaping a conventional, stereotypical adolescence that many youth do not match.

Table 2.1. Rachel's Sample Characterization Chart of Holden Completed with Student Help

Holden's Satirical Characterization of Sex

With your partner or small group, consider Holden's characterization of sex. Consider the narrative techniques used to achieve this characterization, and the way in which this characterization contributes to Holden's. Also think about what Salinger seems to be saying about sex and what society views as normal as it pertains to sex. Identify three to five well-selected passages from the novel that support your interpretation.

How does Holden describe sex? What is being criticized about sex or society's view of sex?	How does Holden's characterization of sex aid in his own characterization?	How does Holden's narrative style contribute to this characterization? (Point to diction, tone, syntax, etc.)	What comment(s) does Salinger seem to be making about sex and what society views as normal as it pertains to sex?	Identify 3–5 passages from the text that support your interpretation and explain how they do so.
Everyone is expected to have sex, particularly teenage males. Sex is casual. Sex is crummy and he has negative feelings about it. He thinks sexual "difference" is perverted. He thinks sex is confusing and he doesn't understand it. He also thinks sex is romantic. He is interested in and excited by sex, but he is also afraid of it and it makes him nervous. **Critiques** Holden criticizes the casual attitude people have toward sex. He criticizes the pressure that society places on males to be sexually virile and display sexual prowess. He criticizes sexual deviance.	The fact that he, as a teen male, is not sexually promiscuous reveals he is different from his peers, and suggests that his sexual conservativeness contributes to his position as an outcast both in his school and in his society. His disgust about the casual way in which sex is treated shows that he refuses to align himself with society's values concerning sex. His characterization of sex as romantic and as something to be shared only between people who are in love shows us that he values emotional intimacy over physical intimacy. The fact that he characterizes sex as both something that confuses him *and* something that excites him suggests that he wants to fit in but cannot bring himself to do what is necessary to be considered "normal."	Holden uses words like "confusing" and "crummy" to describe sex. He uses words like "perverts" and "screwballs" to describe those who are overtly sexual. **Tone** He often uses a critical tone when talking about sex, and always uses a tone full of disgust when talking about sexual deviance and sexual promiscuity. He sometimes uses a confident/boastful tone when describing his own sexuality, but that changes to a shameful and defensive tone when the truth about his lack of sexual experience is revealed. **Syntax** Holden's style and syntax are related in the casual way in which he relates the story. He uses slang and colloquialism and addresses his reader directly.	Society seems to think that people, particularly teen males, should be having a lot of sex with many different partners. Through Holden's criticism of this behavior, Salinger critiques society's shallowness and raises questions about the casual way in which society treats sex. Society sexually objectifies women and lauds accolades on men who are able to demonstrate their masculinity through numerous and frequent sexual conquests. Popularity and social success seem dependent on sexual prowess. Holden's suffering as a result of society's belief that "real" men have sex (a lot of it) allows Salinger to get the reader to see the damaging effects of societal conventions on those who do not want to/are not able to conform to those expectations.	"I know you're supposed to feel pretty sexy when somebody gets up and pulls their dress over their head, but I didn't. Sexy was about the *last* thing I was feeling. I felt much more depressed than sexy" (Salinger p. 95). This demonstrates Holden's discomfort with sex and shows his inner turmoil. On one hand, he is faced with societal expectations—"feel sexy when somebody . . . pulls their dress over their head," but on the other hand, he is tortured by the reality that he doesn't feel the way society expects him to feel, "feeling more depressed than sexy." "If you want to know the truth, I'm a virgin. I really am. I've had quite a few opportunities to lose my virginity and all, but I've never got around to it yet" (Salinger p. 92). Despite his constant boasting about feeling sexy, Holden admits that he is a virgin. Yet he feels the need to justify his status because his society considers it abnormal for an adolescent male to be anything other than a "sexual beast."

"One of the expectations that Holden resists is tied to sex, right? He doesn't think about sex the way that others around him do. Let's look at how Holden talks about sex to see what it reveals about him as a character." Typing into a Word document projected onto a screen, Rachel works with students to fill in a chart about how Holden describes sex. "How does Holden discuss sex?" As several students respond, Rachel types their answers into the chart's first column.

Crummy. Confusing: he has mixed feelings about sex. Romantic. Perverted: he sees people doing strange things through his window and thinks Stradlater would fit in well.

Still typing into the first column of the chart, Rachel asks: "What is he criticizing about sex through these comments?"

It's too casual; it should mean something when people do it. He doesn't like men's roles in sex: it upsets Holden that Stradlater didn't even know Jane's name and he had sex with her.

Shifting to the second column of the chart, Rachel asks, "How do the things he says about sex show us more about him as a character?"

He's not promiscuous. He's phony himself: he's a virgin yet he keeps talking about feeling sexy.

Rachel sees a chance to move students' analyses further toward expectations of male adolescence. She refers the class to Chapter 13 where he divulges his virginity, reading a scene aloud to the class.

> I was starting to feel pretty sexy and all, but I was a little nervous anyway. If you want to know the truth, I'm a virgin. I really am. I've had quite a few opportunities to lose my virginity and all, but I've never got around to it yet. Something always happens. [. . .] I came quite close to doing it a couple of times, though. One time in particular, I remember. Something went wrong, though—I don't even remember what any more. The thing is, most of the time when you're coming pretty close to doing it with a girl —a girl that isn't a prostitute or anything, I mean—she keeps telling you to stop. The trouble with me is, I stop. Most guys don't. I can't help it. You never know whether they really *want* you to stop, or whether they're just scared as hell, or whether they're just telling you to stop so that if you *do* go through with it, the blame'll be on *you*, not them. Anyway, I keep stopping. (p. 92)

Still capturing their responses into the chart, Rachel asks: "Why does he feel the need to justify the fact that he's a virgin? He keeps saying that there's nothing wrong with him. 'I could have done it if I wanted to.' So why explain himself so much?"

Tom replies again: "Social pressure. If he doesn't talk that way, people will think that something is wrong with him."

Rachel reinforces this response: "How are adolescent males like Holden supposed to act?"

Hormonal and freaky. Pushing each other, punching around, talking about what they did with girls.

Now Rachel asks students for a strong passage in the text to support this developing interpretation. Ann, who volunteers at a local hospital after school, reads a scene where Holden is in a room with a very young prostitute: "I know you're supposed to feel pretty sexy when somebody gets up and pulls their dress over their head, but I didn't. *Sexy was about the last thing I was feeling. I felt much more depressed than sexy.*"

Rachel asks the class about the significance of this passage. She captures the ideas of several students into the last column of the chart.

Social pressure has an effect on him. It makes him feel like an outcast, like there's something wrong with him.

Completing the rest of the chart, Rachel summarizes their analyses on this topic: "Holden doesn't fit society's expectations of the adolescent male as sexual."

Giving students a minute to think about this statement, Rachel asks students: "Is Holden just another stereotypical representation of the suffering adolescent, or did Salinger have another purpose by portraying him as he does?" This question is a variation of the central question of the Youth Lens, and one the students would answer in their final assessments in the course: How do texts represent adolescence/ts? Having loosely introduced students to interpretations of Holden as a legitimate protester of uncomfortable, unbefitting sexual expectations of him as a young man, Rachel begins to guide a literary interpretation of this protagonist as suffering not from an adolescence triggered by his body and age, but from social expectations of him as "a male adolescent."

Rachel identified several main topics of repeated concern and complaint by Holden—sex, school and its teachers, parents, other teens, society in general, and himself—and designed a separate chart for each of these topics. Once they completed their charts on the other topics in small groups, students shared their charts, through Google Docs, with the class so everyone could benefit from each other's learning. Designing this activity as a collaborative one makes a lot of sense since it is challenging and since understanding the significance of it would help students really see the impact of the Youth Lens for uncovering a distinct reading of *Catcher* that would also differ substantively from their initial reactions to the novel.

For each topic, students were guided to consider four key questions and to substantiate their responses with textual evidence that they had to explain. I see two of these questions as being integral to understanding a Youth Lens: "How does Holden describe or characterize society (e.g., sex, school, parents, teens, society in general, himself)?" and "What comment/s does Salinger seem to be making about society and what it values as normal?" The other two questions are important for building literary analysis skills about characterization ("How does his description of sex aid in his own characterization?") as well as literary style ("How does his narra-tive style contribute to this characterization?") that support ideas from the Youth Lens as well.

In addition, taken in concert, the six topics that Rachel assembled around which to build this set of charts offer students a glimpse into several of the kinds of analyses that a Youth Lens invites since they focus on key assumptions around adolescents: adolescents as

- governed by hormones (sex),
- dependent on and resistant to adults (parents and schools/teachers) and soci-ety (society in general),
- peer oriented (other teens), and
- self-absorbed (himself).

Through student presentations to each other about their responses and the discus-sions that followed, Rachel planted the seeds for ideas that students could later use to shape an interpretation about the representation of adolescence in *Catcher* for their final essays.

Assessment

The unit culminated in the writing of an essay on *Catcher* in response to a 2008 AP prompt focused on adolescence, as well as the aforementioned formal presen-tations to a university audience of English teachers in training. All students also participated in research interviews with me. Just as it is important to pause at the beginning of the unit to capture students' initial thoughts about adolescence and the central text, designing the unit so it culminates with opportunities to reflect on any shifts—or resistances—in thinking about these ideas can be very revealing. Through the AP essay on *Catcher* and adolescence, through student presentations at the university, and through my interviews, students had ample opportunity to think about their learning during the unit.

The AP exam prompt read as follows:

> In some works of literature, childhood and adolescence are portrayed as times graced by innocence and a sense of wonder; in other works, they are depicted as times of tribulation and terror. Focusing on a single novel or play, explain how its representa-tion of childhood or adolescence shapes the meaning of the work as a whole. (The College Board, 2008)

In many ways, this prompt is perfect for this unit given its focus on representations of adolescence. However, it bears note that, read conventionally, the prompt seems to hold to dominant views of adolescence, especially the echo of common descriptive language for this social category in the phrase "times of tribulation and terror." I would argue that this setup in the prompt makes the essay more challenging for students attempting to apply a Youth Lens to their interpretation of the novel. Teachers who decide to try out a prompt like this might either revise it or draw attention to the ways it relies on stereotypical views of youth. Additionally, teachers could ask students to critique the prompt itself through their emerging knowledge of adolescence as a construct, and these responses would serve as complementary evidence of students' learning in the unit.

In Rachel's class, through process-based—rather than timed—writing, students responded to this prompt in essay form for *The Catcher in the Rye*. Student Dominique's opening to her thesis shows the way she chose to interpret the prompt's positioning of adolescence as potentially tumultuous: "Holden is in a constant period of tribulation and terror because he rejects all that society imposes on him. He refuses to assimilate or conform to the 'norms' of society and the rules of a typical adolescent." According to Dominique, if adolescence reflects tumult it is because of the strain of fighting social pressure to fit into narrow behaviors expected of youth. Rather than see the tumult as a result of the *natural* stage of adolescence, Dominique applies ideas of a *historically situated* adolescence to show that sometimes when we see youth struggling, it is not a sign of natural rebelliousness but, rather, legitimate social resistance to unappealing or impossible norms. Another student, Nicole, who would end up writing her senior project on the discrimination of youth, also attributed Holden's suffering to social pressure affixed to narrow norms for youth. In her thesis statement, Nicole asserted:

> Holden's bitter somber life is no accident: With a buildup of social pressures which include struggles with masculinity and the ensuing loneliness, he embodies what it is like to be a victim of the tribulation and terror caused by a society that values conformity more than anything else.

Though Nicole doesn't repeat the fact that "tribulation and terror" is intended to characterize adolescence in the prompt to which she responds, her thesis shows that readers ought to see Holden's suffering as predictable—"no accident"—as an understandable reaction to being a specific kind of adolescent male. In other words, Nicole characterizes Holden as a "victim" of dominant expectations of adolescence.

As a second culminating assessment to this unit, students presented their learning about adolescence and about applying a Youth Lens to *Catcher* to a university audience of preservice teachers. The university students were also studying adolescence and applying a Youth Lens to literature, but in their case, it was to YAL for a course I was teaching. Rachel's students knew about these presentations from the start of the unit, and she situated them as opportunities for her students to showcase their learning to an audience of people who could change the ways that young people were thought about and treated in schools. Students were nervous about and motivated by this opportunity.

In their individual and group presentations, students shared work from all the parts of the curriculum discussed so far. They discussed their initial ideas about adolescence, echoing dominant views about youth, and their initial views of Holden read through these dominant views of adolescence: He's a whiny wimp. They also demonstrated their new knowledge about adolescence, sharing their understanding of what it means to think of adolescence as a construct. Their presentations closed with examples of how their new ideas of adolescence affected their literary interpretations and their ideas about the world, teachers, and themselves.

Tom's ideas represent some of the ways students commented on the impact of the unit.

> Whenever you see teens in a movie, in most cases, they're partying and drinking and experimenting with drugs and sex. Now I see it as societal rather than "Why are these kids so crazy?" I thought it just happened that way when they turn thirteen; now I see it as, "when you turn thirteen, this is how you fit in." I don't hang around people who party; it's not in my interest. I hang around people who are my friends, who play video games and listen to rock music. I found a safe net away from the popular crowd.

Tom's reflections on his learning through the unit point to a shift from a naturalized view of adolescence to one that is culturally constructed: "This is how you fit in." And this shift in thinking explains or justifies his choice to avoid a popularity that he sees as unsavory and as plagued by pressures to fit within narrow social expectations for youth.

Other students, like Atticus, who loves to swim at the local YMCA four times a week and play heavy metal guitar in his free time, discussed his new view of the role of schools in youths' lives.

> In school we are taught how to function in society and take on the tasks it gives us without question. This suggests that the function of school is [not] education but to train students to become model citizens, to get students to accept ideas as their own, when in reality, they were implanted over years of subjectification. After being exposed to this idea, I didn't feel like the idea of what I wanted to be was my own but more like a pawn on a chessboard. Without this lens, I would not have seen Holden from *The Catcher in the Rye* as an adolescent who couldn't conform to what society wanted. Adolescence is shown to be a life stage where one is shown how to fit into society and if one fails to learn, he is faced with alienation and loneliness.

In his pretty sobering view of life, Atticus outlines the pressure that schools put on youth to fit social norms through a key term, *subjectification*, learned through his class's reading of a research article on adolescence.

The culminating interviews with me also revealed a lot about how much students were thinking about the implications of these ideas on adolescence in their lives. I could easily imagine a class wherein students interviewed each other to prompt such insights, maybe even crafting a journalistic video news story about these shifts to be shared with others. (See Chapter 5 for more assessment ideas.) In their interviews with me, students identified facets of "dominant adolescence" in films, the things their parents and other adults said to and about them, and in their peers' actions. And they were infuriated about these representations.

Dominique, a state-ranked athlete, disapproved of the ways her peers presented themselves on social media. Like many of the students, Dominique was connected through social media with her parents and other adults as well as with younger family members, so when other youth at her school or in the community posted status changes about their sex lives or images of provocative piercings, Dominique balked. "You have family members as friends on Facebook. Do you really want to post these types of statuses? I go and hide other people's statuses and their pictures because I don't want people seeing my newsfeed with it." Commenting on her peers' reflection of stereotypes tied to sexuality, Dominique distanced herself from them and their reflection of stereotypes tied to a hormone-governed adolescence which she rejected. In ways that will be discussed further in Chapter 4, in these comments, we can also see that Dominique prioritizes her family—in addition to her commitment to athletic achievement—much more than her peers. Through a statement like this, Dominique explicitly critiques conventional versions of adolescence as hormone-crazed, and implicitly shows that not all teens are peer-obsessed to the exclusion of their interest in and respect for the adults and non-teens in their own families and communities.

For some students like Julio, who came into the class questioning dominant ideas supporting the status quo, this curriculum reinforced points of social critique that he already believed about how powerful groups dominate less powerful groups. For others like Tom and Atticus (the latter of whom chose his pseudonym after first wanting to use Holden since he, like Tom, identified with him so much), learning that adolescence was not always thought about the way we do today relieved them of some of the pressure of feeling inadequate for not fitting social norms of adolescent masculinity. "I grew up in this unit," Tom stated unironically.

But not all students were convinced. From the unit's beginning to its end, Alexandris, a student who identified as popular in her school—different from how most of the others in the class self-identified—found the idea of adolescence as a cultural construct difficult to believe. Alexandris repeatedly pointed to the many students all over their school and in their community who behaved *exactly* like "teens" or "adolescents": recklessly, experimenting with sex and drugs, going out late and breaking curfews. Even after Rachel explained that they might be doing so because they are fitting the norm of what is expected of them, Alexandris resisted this knowledge. To me, in her final interview comments, she explained why she remained resistant: She has a hard time changing her mind unless there is abundant proof, and trying to do so without what she considers sufficient evidence feels like an insult to her intelligence. No one likes to feel that they have been wrong in their thinking. Any curriculum that aims to change students' minds risks alienating those same youths. Perhaps, for this reason, in Rachel's class this curriculum proved most transformative for the students left out of dominant views of adolescence either because of race, class, or strict parents who restricted their social lives. Yet interestingly, when I asked, in the final interview, if the curriculum was worthwhile for other youth, too, even Alexandris recommended this curriculum: "Yeah, I think everyone should do it. It gets the ball rolling. It's a great way to show you what you haven't seen before. Puts the world in a new light."

Ideas for Trying This Out

- Gather a range of popular texts featuring youth to analyze how adolescence is represented to invite students to begin to draw attention to the ways youth are typically—and atypically—portrayed.

  - How do a range of song lyrics—and their videos—portray youth? Peter Tosh's "Can't Blame the Youth" works very well to show how young people are being taught by adults to believe in problematic myths and then blamed for their problematic beliefs. In a very different rendering of adolescence in relation to adults, Belle & Sebastian's "Me and the Major" focuses on the differences between a young man and "the major" who wants to enlist him in the Queen's army to make a man of him. In this song—as with many songs—adolescence or youth is what adults miss or are nostalgic for now that they are adults living unhappy lives. In other words, adults try to "enlist" youth to follow an unhappy path to a conventional adulthood that they occupy. What other songs or music videos might you employ to analyze and evaluate adolescence in music?

  - Ask students to examine any favorite or popular television or online shows featuring youth. What kinds of activities consume their attention? How do they speak? Do they have jobs, and if so, is their pay designated for recreational or bill-paying purposes? In what kinds of spaces do young people gather (e.g., outdoors, in malls, in homes, rural/urban) and how are they seen in these spaces, especially by adults? What are the races of the youth featured? When you compare youth of different races—and classes—across programming, what do you notice? For more on launching a media-based unit that examines representations of and invites new media productions of young people, see Chapter 3.

- Examine the range of literary texts you teach for representations of adolescence to consider variations in and intersections of race, gender, sexuality, class, religion, and age, as well as the social context—and time period—in which the text was written.

  - What does "adolescence" look like in texts that were written before the period when the category of adolescence that we have inherited today—the 1890s–1920s—was constructed? For example, what do readers notice when rethinking Shakespeare's *Romeo and Juliet* through a Youth Lens? Do Romeo and Juliet reflect typical traits of adolescence that we would expect today? Is that how their actions are interpreted? Or does Shakespeare provide a more complex context through which their haste to marry and their fierce love for each other is to be seen? Which other canonical texts typically read in English classes can be revisited with questions stemming from a Youth Lens in mind?

  - What does "adolescence" look like in texts featuring raced or classed youth, for example? Groenke et al. (2015) raise some enormously important questions about whether black youth are even permitted an adolescence. Through this question, these scholars point to the fact that, even though adolescence functions as a diminished social category for many youth, especially in relation to adulthood, for some it remains a privileged category unavailable to them. For example, when reading Walter Dean Myers's *Monster*, how do the various media through which Steve Harmon's story is told—his journal, the screenplay, and the photographs and courtroom sketches—portray Steve? If seen through the photographs— the grainy renderings that match news media images of youth caught on security camera, or the shots of Steve in a jail cell out of clear focus—Steve appears guilty by virtue of matching him visually with other guilty parties in media representations of black youth. If Steve is analyzed through the journal, his expressions of fear, despondency, and desperation make him appear much more vulnerable. The screenplay pushes him into the third person without the kind of explanation available through the journal (to explain, for example, that his attendance at Stuyvesant High School—a top-ranked, competitive public school in Manhattan—means that he is a very good student), which adds another complex layer to his rendering. But these representations together are all written by Steve (and Myers, of course), so he is managing his representation through all of them, thereby adding to the complexity of his depiction. Using a text like this in relation to texts featuring White or Asian or Latinx youth will help to offer students a chance to interrogate adolescence as a raced category and reconsider the implications of this assumption. See Chapter 4 for more ideas about how to employ a Youth Lens with YAL in general, and with *Monster* as one specific example.

Closing Thoughts

For teachers motivated to identify more ways to engage students in literary study, especially students who may feel left out of the curriculum, taking up a Youth Lens through which to study literary and media texts—and even youths' lives in and outside school—may offer fresh avenues for reviving the literacy curriculum for a much broader range of young people.

"It's like adults think we're brain dead. Are we brain dead?" High School Students Critiquing and Creating Representations of Youth in the Media

Robert Petrone

In the Classroom

Amid posters of Edgar Allan Poe, William Faulkner, Alice Walker, Robert Frost, Ernest Hemingway, and a range of other canonical authors, images of teenagers cover the walls of Bethany's eleventh-grade English classroom. These images include advertisements from magazines; printouts of websites, cartoons, and comics; screenshots of TV commercials; and pictures of musicians and characters from popular films and TV shows. They are taped to the walls around the room in five groupings, each of which is organized under one of the following headings: "Immature," "Social," "Party Goers," "Sexual," and "Self-absorbed/Self-image."

These images, and the categories under which they are located, are the result of an assignment from the beginning of a four-week unit titled "Media Representations of Youth." As will be discussed in more detail throughout this chapter, this unit moved students through a process of first examining and critiquing media texts for depictions of young people, and then creating their own media texts in order to more comprehensively represent youth.

The homework assignment from the introductory lesson of the unit was simply for students to find examples of teenagers in the media and bring those texts to the subsequent class session. The next day, the students analyzed the images in small groups, and then as a whole class, they established broader categories that embodied the main ideas being conveyed through these images. So, for example, all of the images that depicted eroticized youth were grouped together and given the heading "Sexual." Similarly, all of the images that showed young

continued on next page

people drinking alcohol or smoking cigarettes were grouped together under the heading "Party Goers."

Once the class established these categories (and physically tacked the images on the walls about the room), the teacher, Bethany (pseudonym), asked the students to write on and be prepared to discuss the following question for homework that night: "What is the media saying about youth and young people?"

And thus, the students began their four-week inquiry into media representations of youth—what many of them would indicate at the end of the year was a particularly engaging unit since it was, as one student said, "something that pertained to us." The remainder of this chapter explains this unit in detail, providing some context of the school and students, the overarching aims and sequences of activities of the unit, as well as some ideas on how to think beyond what was done in this unit to adapt to your own teaching situation.

School Context

Bethany was first introduced to the idea of adolescence as a construct during her undergraduate teacher preparation program and then through professional development (i.e., a regional professional conference). Interested in trying the idea out during her first year of teaching, she contacted me (Rob), her former university professor, to develop a unit focused on media representations of adolescence and youth as part of her eleventh-grade English class. Bethany's impetus in designing the unit was to create a space in the curriculum where her students could "see themselves," as she said, and engage with content in a way they otherwise might not get the opportunity to in a traditional English class. Her hypothesis was that creating a unit focused on examining how youth get represented in media would increase motivation for students—something she later attested was exactly what happened. In an interview with me at the end of the year, she explained that student engagement was higher during this particular unit than in others, describing that she saw students who had previously been "out of it" in terms of engagement and participation really "jump back into" the class and "click" with the curriculum in this unit.

Having long had an interest in critical media literacy, Bethany conceptualized merging the idea of adolescence as socially constructed with media literacy, and hence the idea for this particular unit was hatched. Over the course of several months, we collaborated on developing the curriculum, and then over the span of four weeks, Bethany taught it while I had the opportunity to observe many of the lessons as well as interview the students about their experiences with it.

Centennial High School (a pseudonym; hereafter CHS) is an interesting place. Though it is located in a region typically known as one of the most rural and remote in the country, it is one of the largest schools in the area (approximately

1,200 students) and situated in one of the largest communities in the region (approximately 70,000 people), the center of which is a major state university. This creates a mix of students across a wide range of socioeconomic statuses, as well as rural, suburban, and even urban identifications. The racial breakdown of the student population includes White (91%), American Indian (3%), Latinx (2%), Asian (1.5%), African American (1.5%), and Other (1%). Of the twenty-three students in this particular eleventh-grade class, two identify as African American and one as Latinx. Twenty-three percent of students at the school are eligible for free and reduced lunch, and 95 percent of students graduate. Bethany is a twenty-three-year-old White woman who graduated from CHS just five years prior to her first year of teaching there, and I am a White, male English education professor at a state university.

Theory: Critical Media Literacy

As a former high school English language arts teacher and current English education professor, I have long held the belief that an important component of secondary English curriculum ought to be teaching about media. Over the years, I have come to understand that one way to do this is through the integration of media texts into the curriculum to augment other, more established, textual activities. For example, in a curriculum I developed with a different teacher, we used clips of Disney films to teach literary lenses (Appleman, 2015), such as a feminist lens, that students then applied to their analyses of John Steinbeck's *Of Mice and Men*. (See Petrone & Borsheim [2008] for a description of this curriculum, which includes many other examples of integrating media texts to facilitate more traditional academic textual activities, including elements of satire, rhetorical analysis, and writing the research paper.)

A second way of bringing media into the English classroom is through the explicit teaching of media literacy whereby students explore how to read and write media texts themselves. Because media are such a powerful presence—for better and for worse—in our everyday lives, the English classroom can function as a space to examine these texts for their implicit and explicit messages and persuasive techniques. Doing so helps us all become more savvy consumers and producers of media. The need for increased attention to media texts within secondary English is even more urgent at this time given the proliferation of digital technologies that increasingly make media texts the primary literacy tasks of our contemporary work, social relations, and personal lives.

This second method to integrating media in the English curriculum is typically referred to as critical media literacy (e.g., Kellner & Share, 2005; Morrell, Deuñas, Garcia, & López, 2013). A critical media literacy is a particular approach to consuming, producing, and disseminating media texts. This approach foregrounds issues of representation in media texts, particularly troubling depictions of social categories such as race, class, gender, sexuality, dis/ability, urban, rural, and other social identifications. More specifically, critical media literacy has two central aims: (1) to help students read, or deconstruct, media images to examine how they work to perpetuate particular ideas; and (2) to aid students in creating media texts that provide more comprehensive, balanced perspectives. See Table 3.1 for a summary of these approaches to teaching media.

Because media texts themselves are typically multimodal, the processes involved in consuming and producing them often involve complex relationships between reading, listening, viewing, writing, speaking/singing, designing, and shooting and editing video. In this way, critical media literacy often extends beyond traditional notions of print-based literacy and works well to make the English curriculum more diverse and representative of students' literacy lives outside of schools.

Up to now, literacy educators have done great work with secondary students to critique and rewrite problematic representations of many social categories, especially class, gender, race, sexuality, and dis/ability through a range of media textual practices. For example, leading media literacy scholar and past NCTE president, Ernest Morrell, and some of his colleagues (Morrell et al., 2013) demonstrate how a group of urban teachers use critical media literacy to help students better

Table 3.1. Central Aims of Critical Media Literacy

Approaches to Media in the English Classroom	Explanation/Example
Integrating media to augment traditional academic literacies	• Uses Disney films to teach literary lenses See, for example, Petrone & Borsheim (2008).
Explicit teaching of critical media literacy	• Analyzes media texts for messages about social categories such as race, class, gender • Creates, revises, and disseminates media texts to offer more comprehensive and realistic representations of social categories See, for example, Morrell et al. (2013).
Critical media literacy that focuses on representations of *youth* and *adolescence*	• Emphasizes how the media helps construct ideas and images of youth and adolescence • Creates a space for youth to create and disseminate media texts to provide more accurate and comprehensive depictions of youth In addition to this chapter, see also Bruce (2015).

understand and redress issues such as racism, violence, and poverty within urban contexts.

However, an area that has not received as much attention when it comes to critical media literacy is how media represent youth and adolescence as social categories. As we suggest in Chapter 1, focusing on the social categories of youth and adolescence is crucial given how dominant views of youth often position young people in diminished ways that have negative effects on their lives.

The unit of study described in this chapter responds directly to this need within the teaching of English by focusing on adolescence and youth. A critical media literacy interwoven with a Youth Lens can help secondary students deconstruct and revise these depictions of youth and adolescence. This approach is especially important given media's particular interest in influencing young people, specifically teenagers, who historically have been a prime audience for marketers (Dretzin & Goodman, 2001; Schor, 2005). In fact, the term *teenager* was introduced into the English language through the marketing sector in the United States in the 1940s—a fact that was actually taught explicitly in this unit of study.

The Curriculum

Goals of the Unit

In Bethany's unit, the students analyzed, discussed, and created a wide range of media texts. Drawing from her own understandings of critical media literacy, knowledge of her students, the standard eleventh-grade curriculum for her school, the school culture, and the broader community, Bethany developed and used the following objectives as guides for the unit:

Textual Consumption (reading, listening, viewing)

1. Students will analyze representations of adolescence/ts and youth in various media formats and the accuracy of those representations.
2. Students will explore and analyze a variety of rhetorical strategies to determine an author's point of view and possible purposes for her/his representation of adolescence and youth.

Prior to this unit, the students had worked on rhetorical analysis in written and literary texts, so Bethany saw this as a great opportunity for them to transfer their knowledge and skills to a different medium.

Textual Production (designing, videography, writing, speaking)

3. Students will use a variety of media formats to create their own representations of youth and adolescence/ts in society.
4. Students will reflect on and be able to articulate the rhetorical moves/strategies they make in creating their texts and the purposes for these moves.

In addition to her own unit objectives, and as mandated by her school, Bethany also linked her unit of study to several English Language Arts Common Core State Standards.

1. CCSS.ELA-LITERACY.RI.11-12.6: Determine an author's point of view or purpose in a text in which the rhetoric is particularly effective, analyzing how style and content contribute to the power, persuasiveness or beauty of the text.

2. CCSS.ELA-LITERACY.RI.11-12.4: Determine the meaning of words and phrases as they are used in a text, including figurative, connotative, and technical meanings; analyze how an author uses and refines the meaning of a key term or terms over the course of a text (e.g., how Madison defines faction in Federalist No. 10).

3. CCSS.ELA-LITERACY.SL.11-12.2: Integrate multiple sources of information presented in diverse formats and media (e.g., visually, quantitatively, orally) in order to make informed decisions and solve problems, evaluating the credibility and accuracy of each source and noting any discrepancies among the data.

4. CCSS.ELA-LITERACY.SL.11-12.3: Evaluate a speaker's point of view, reasoning, and use of evidence and rhetoric, assessing the stance, premises, links among ideas, word choice, points of emphasis, and tone used.

Structure of the Unit

Each of the four weeks of the unit had an overarching focus and corresponding set of activities (see Table 3.2). These weekly plans were arranged to build on one another and help students develop the enabling skills and knowledge they would need to successfully complete the final project: the creation of a media text of their own featuring youth and adolescence that demonstrated their understandings of concepts learned throughout the unit. Specifically, week one provided the foundation for concepts such as media, media literacy, adolescence as a construct, and youth stereotypes. From this conceptual and theoretical base, week two helped students move from ideas of adolescence as a construct and media literacy to examining media's role in developing and perpetuating stereotypes of youth. In this way, week two built on the work of week one. Once students gained comfort with analyzing these pervasive and dominant stereotypical media texts and images, they built on these skills in week three to instead focus on nondominant, positive images of youth in the media. Not only did this week extend their analytic skills developed in the previous weeks, but it also helped them conceptually begin preparing for the final week, which involved them creating their own media text to either critique dominant media images of youth or to illuminate more positive depictions of youth. In these ways, the unit supported students from being consumers of media to producers of media.

Table 3.2. Weekly Summary of Unit

Week One Intro to Media Literacy and Youth Stereotypes	• What is media? Media literacy? • What is a "construct"? How is youth a construct? • What are stereotypes of youth?
Week Two Creation, Pervasiveness, and Consequences of Stereotypical Depictions of Youth in Media	• How do media rely on, perpetuate, and/or create ideas and stereotypes of youth? • What are consequences of these stereotypical depictions of youth?
Week Three Positive and Alternative Depictions of Youth in Media	• How and when are youth portrayed positively in the media? • How do media created by youth differ from adult-generated media in their depictions of youth?
Week Four Re-presenting Youth in the Media	• How might students create media texts to critique dominant images of youth in the media? • How might students create media texts that portray youth in more positive, comprehensive ways?

Texts for the Unit

From these overarching unit goals, Bethany developed a preliminary text set—being sure to keep it open for student selections and contributions—and then a scope and sequence for the unit. Over the course of the four-week unit, the students viewed, read, listened to, analyzed, and discussed a wide range of media texts, including websites, blogs, social media, music, music videos, documentaries, newspaper articles, cartoons and illustrations, TV shows, films, and advertisements. In addition, students read and discussed excerpts from literary texts in order to link their analyses of media to more traditionally taught texts, such as novels, helping them see how ideas of youth and adolescence circulate not only in media but also in literature—both canonical and those designated Young Adult. (See Chapters 2 and 4 for further discussion of the Youth Lens and approaches to analyzing literary texts for depictions of youth and adolescence.) Some of the specific texts used in this unit include:

- *Merchants of Cool* (2001), PBS documentary. Students viewed and discussed a fifteen-minute clip related to the concept of the "feedback loop." The feedback loop, as explained in the documentary, is a process whereby media companies research youth to figure out what's "cool," then amplify it and market it to sell back to youth. In time, the media industry moves from merely reflecting back to youth to actually creating youth culture for consumption all the while claiming it is just mirroring back to youth who they are.

- TV commercial for Totino's Pizza Rolls
  http://www.youtube.com/watch?v=41Vx8AlLQOQ
- TV commercial for Allstate Insurance
  https://www.youtube.com/watch?v=vtP-S9OS0o0
- Clip from a *Dr. Drew* episode on the "Teenage Brain"
  http://www.hlntv.com/video/2012/09/04/why-are-teens-so-predisposed-risk-taking-behavior
- *New Yorker* cartoons on adolescence
- *Huffington Post* article, "The Teenage Brain: Debunking the Five Biggest Myths"
  http://www.huffingtonpost.com/david-moshman/adolescents-and-their-tee_b_858360.html
- Opening chapters of *The Absolutely True Diary of a Part-Time Indian*, *The Catcher in the Rye*, *Looking for Alaska*, and *Twilight*
- Newspaper (print and digital) articles and blogs on high school students protesting standardized testing
- Articles and blog posts on research conducted in the United Kingdom on the effects that media depictions of youth have on their employment opportunities
- Documentary produced by students at CHS a few years prior investigating the school district superintendent's pay raise. This text was used to locate more positive representations of youth, as well as the ways adults tend to minimize youth contributions and inquiries.
- A wide range of other media texts both generated by the students (their own media texts) and texts they would bring into the class for discussion (as evidenced in the vignette at the beginning of the chapter).

Approaches to Examining and Producing Media Texts

Beyond text selection, an important consideration for a unit on examining media is figuring out and working with students on approaches to analyzing (and ultimately producing) media texts. Given the critical media literacy theoretical framework for the unit that foregrounds issues of problematic representations of social categories (in this case, youth and adolescence), Bethany felt it was crucial to work with students on the idea of media being constructed, and as such, reflecting ideologies that promote particular viewpoints on youth and adolescence. From this perspective, Bethany adapted the Center for Media Literacy's five core concepts and key questions (www.medialit.org) as central ideas to frame the entire unit.

Core Concepts for Media Literacy

1. All media messages are constructed.
2. Media messages are constructed using a creative language with its own rules.
3. Different people experience the same media message differently.
4. Media have embedded values and points of view.
5. Most media messages are organized to gain profit and/or power.

While these core concepts served as a useful entry point for discussion of media texts and industries in general, additional key questions functioned as an important heuristic for the students to draw on as they analyzed and constructed media texts. Taking the Center for Media Literacy's five original questions, Bethany added two questions of her own, and nuanced the original questions to better fit the language of the class and align with previously learned content about rhetoric (e.g., ethos, pathos, logos). What follows is the adapted set of questions Bethany provided the students:

Key Questions for Media Literacy

1. Who created this message? [Author]
   a. Who is the author?
   b. What is their background? What is their "agenda"/goal?
2. What creative techniques are used to *attract my attention*?
3. What strategies are used *to convince or persuade* me to think a certain way or to take a certain action?
   a. Ethos (credibility)
   b. Logos (logic)
   c. Pathos (emotion)
4. To whom is this media targeted/for? [Intended Audience]
   a. What creative techniques are being used to target/attract the intended audience?
   b. What rhetorical strategies are being used to convince/persuade the audience?
   c. What assumptions is the author making about the intended audience?
5. What values, lifestyles, and points of view are represented in, or omitted from, this message?
6. How might different people understand this message differently? [Audience Interpretation]
7. Why is this message being sent? [Purpose]

These questions pushed students to take into consideration many issues related to author and audience. Because so much media aimed at youth is produced by adults, students questioned the authenticity of these particular depictions of youth. They wondered what differences would arise if these depictions of youth were created by youth themselves. They also posed questions about adult agendas through the media, including attempts to manipulate youth as consumers. Overall, students expressed interest and even concern as to *who* was using the media to tell them who and how they were supposed to be as youth and adolescents.

These concerns about authors and intended audiences of media texts became an important and generative theme for the entire unit. Ultimately, this area of analysis led to discussions about the role of other adults in the students' lives, including parents and teachers. In fact, a fair number of final projects drew on these sets of relationships to offer critiques of representations of youth—and adults. (See a discussion of peer-orientation in Chapter 4 for more on this topic.)

The seven questions above, originally given to the students as a heuristic, ultimately became a starting point for students to modify and make their own. Over the course of the unit, students generated additional, often more nuanced, interpretive questions such as the following:

- How are the relationships between youth and adults characterized?
- Are youth positioned as authorities? as in need of authority? as deviant?
- Are youth represented as being hormonal?
- How are peer-to-peer interactions portrayed?

Beginning with questions as an approach to understanding and critiquing media texts not only helped the students analyze particular texts but also pushed their meta-thinking about how to go about analyzing media texts in general. Thus, this unit not only facilitated the students' understanding of the content but, more important, it also engaged them in a process of critique in which they were active participants.

Key Activities

From Media Literacy in General to Depictions of Youth in the Media

Bethany began the first day with an advertisement for AXE dandruff shampoo—both to orient the students to media literacy and to practice with the heuristic she had developed for them to use throughout the unit. The left side of the ad contains a picture of two bottles of AXE shampoo with the following words above it: "Lose the Flakes, Get the Girls." The right side of the advertisement contains a photo of a guy with no shirt on, holding two bottles of the shampoo, with two women, dressed in towels, looking at him, their hands on his shoulders and chest. The women have sexually suggestive looks on their faces and the man is smiling.

Bethany had the ad on the LCD projector as the students shuffled into the class and led a discussion related to the purposes, audiences, and (problematic) messages in the ad. From there, she introduced critical media literacy and the heuristic questions and then provided the students with several more sample ads to begin their analysis of media in small groups. From these small groups, Bethany brought the class together to talk across their examples to illuminate the above definitions of critical media literacy. From this first day activity, Bethany asked students to find and bring into class the next day examples of media depictions of youth, which culminated in the activity described at the beginning of the chapter.

Adolescence as a Construct

On the second day, Bethany introduced the general idea of a social construct before moving to a more specific discussion of the key ideas in the unit: that both the media and youth/adolescence are social constructs. She did this by drawing on some concepts the class had previously studied when reading Tim O'Brien's collection of stories about soldiers' experiences before, during, and after the Vietnam War in *The Things They Carried*—namely, the idea of masculinity as a social construct. Starting, then, with this previous experience and class lexicon, Bethany used an interactive PowerPoint presentation including video clips and discussions to teach about adolescence as a social construct.

Her goal was to illustrate how the experience of being a teenager is not fixed or natural but dependent on social context. To explain the idea of meaning being imbued by context and not inherent in something, she started with weather. For instance, she asked students to explain if the snow and rain were "good" or "bad." This prompt generated discussion about how in certain instances snow was desirable (e.g., if you are snowboarding), whereas other times it was undesirable (e.g., if you have to drive your car to work). She then talked about different playing cards and asked if they were "good" or "bad" cards to have in your hand. The students, of course, explained that it depended on what game you were playing and the circumstances of that particular hand. From these examples, she then moved on to how meanings of concepts such as teenagers and adolescence are dependent on circumstances rather than having inherent meaning.

Specifically, she examined how ideas of adolescence are always shaped by particular social circumstances rather than a universally experienced stage of life governed by biology and psychology. One of the approaches she used to illustrate this was by explaining how sixteen-year-olds (the age of many of the students) have been understood differently at different historical moments and cultural contexts. So, for example, she explained how sixteen-year-olds in 1850 were parents, business owners, and so on, whereas today, though sixteen-year-olds could be parents, it was nonnormative for them to be so, and that today, sixteen-year-olds were often understood as "students" and "teenagers." She explained how even the word *teenager* is a relatively new term, only appearing in the English language in 1941. She also explained how being sixteen years old in different cultures—and even across different socioeconomic groups within the United States—was a different experience. (Many of the ideas and examples Bethany used in her presentation are discussed in Chapters 1 and 4 in this book, as well as in Borsheim-Black [2015].)

Establishing Dominant Depictions of Youth in the Media

From the idea that youth and adolescence are social constructs, Bethany helped students ascertain a sense of what dominant, or "normal" ideas of youth and adolescence were circulating in mainstream media. To begin this inquiry, she invited students to bring in an array of media texts from their lives (e.g., films, social media, websites, TV shows) and then discuss and analyze them in class. For instance, students brought in the opening clip of the movie *Clueless* and a clip of a cafeteria scene from *Mean Girls*—both are films that focus on teenage life through female protagonists and rely on and critique many stereotypes of youth. They also brought in articles and advertisements from teen magazines, some of which focused on beauty products, and anti-smoking campaigns targeted at teens. From these texts, the students ascertained that the normal ideas of youth the media promoted were nearly all deficit-oriented and positioned youth as partiers, as well as apathetic, rebellious, sexual, and, overall, out of control.

Building on these findings, Bethany brought explicit attention to the idea of the "teenage brain" as a prevailing characterization of youth. Specifically, Bethany and the students read, viewed, and discussed a set of *New Yorker* cartoons, an episode of the *Dr. Drew Show*, and a *Huffington Post* article (all discussed in Chapter 1, as well). The exploration culminated in the viewing and discussion of the *Dr. Drew Show* clip from an episode that cohered around the question: Why are teenagers so prone to risky behavior? The episode featured an expert on the topic, Dr. Gail Saltz, an associate professor of psychiatry at New York Presbyterian Hospital and author of the book *Anatomy of a Secret Life*. In the clip, Dr. Saltz explained how teenagers, because of their brains, were not able to control themselves. "The [frontal lobe] is the part of your brain that houses consequence and judgment. So the idea, 'If I do this today what will happen to me tomorrow,' that's not fully there for a teenager." In response, Dr. Drew, the show's host, ran a pointer over a graphic of a "teen brain," and said, in part: "The frontal lobe, the prefrontal cortex, shuts down for remodeling. It literally shuts down—doesn't function. Adolescents are actually relying on you, the adults' frontal lobe, to superimpose on them to protect them."

After watching this short clip, Bethany opened up the lesson for discussion. Though the students were regularly engaged in whole-group discussions throughout the unit, they were particularly so in this one. Right away, hands shot into the air and students began talking. Several expressed their being offended by the clip and the ideas contained in it, particularly the vehemence with which the adults on the show expressed them. "The video says that part of our brain completely shuts off during adolescence and that accounts for reasons why teens can't make wise decisions," one student said. "I find that statistic a little insulting. I personally think I can make good decisions." Another student, exasperated, said: "It's like adults think we're brain dead. Are we brain dead?" From there, several others chimed in, and the conversation continued with students talking about interactions they've had with adults—in schools, in stores and malls and public spaces, and in their homes, too. The undercurrent to nearly all of their examples was that they felt consistently disrespected or otherwise treated unfairly because of their age and status as teenagers. In other words, for them, the rhetoric from the TV show clip was consonant with their lived experiences.

From Media to Literature and Schools

Once they established dominant media representations of youth, Bethany and the students examined depictions of youth in literary texts and even their own school. Specifically, Bethany developed an activity in which students had to tour their school and community and photograph various ways youth were being understood, positioned, and represented within it. The students came back with photos, for instance, of spaces in the school, such as faculty lounges, that were off limits to students, as well as pictures of soda machines to indicate how they were being positioned as consumers in their school. This activity helped several students develop ideas for their final projects, as several of them wanted to critique how schools helped perpetuate negative ideas of youth, particularly related to cliques.

Another activity included reading the opening chapters of canonical and young adult literary texts to explore how these texts, too, were depicting youth. They discussed, for instance, Junior, the narrator in Sherman Alexie's *The Absolutely True Diary of a Part-Time Indian*. In this young adult novel about the experiences of an American Indian youth who leaves his reservation to attend the nearby white high school during his ninth-grade year, Junior seemed to assume very normative ways of making sense of himself as a teen boy, particularly through his preoccupation with sex and masturbation. They also discussed the narrators in both *The Catcher in the Rye* (discussed in Chapter 2) and *Looking for Alaska*, a novel about a year in the life of sixteen-year-old Pudge, a white male student who attends a boarding school for the first time. *Looking for Alaska* chronicles Pudge's experiences

of friendships, drinking and smoking cigarettes, loss and grief, and adult authority. In a year-end interview, one student noted this to be his favorite activity in the
unit as it helped illuminate the irony in how negative ideas of youth get packaged
for youths' consumption in texts intended for them as readers. He said, "I really
liked, and I hadn't really thought about it, when we were shown examples in books
that ironically enough [laughs] are targeted toward us but have all these stereotypes
about youth that are not really good." (See Chapter 4 for much more on representations of youth in young adult literature.)

Providing Counter, Positive Portrayals of Youth in the Media

For Bethany, having her students critique dominant media images was not enough.
An important aspect of this unit for her was to both see and create more positive,
comprehensive depictions of youth in the media. To achieve this, Bethany devised
a two-day lesson whereby students read and discussed articles about high school-
ers across the country protesting the standardized tests they were mandated to take
by their districts. The articles showcased youth being interviewed and articulating
their critiques of the testing, particularly in light of how the tests take away from
their instructional time and thus ironically inhibit their learning. During these
two days, students in the class discussed, among other things, their rights as youth.
They debated whether or not they even had the right to protest at all since they
were "underage," as they said. Interestingly, one student applied this discussion to
the media coverage of the Baltimore riots that were occurring at the same time as
the unit. For her, this activity shifted her analysis of media coverage of the riots in
that she started noticing who—adults or youth—was being covered in the media,
and what role youth had in that cause. She explained: "Mostly on the news you see
the adults trying to speak their words and what they think and there's never really
any, any input from teenagers and what their input is."

   This provided Bethany with an opportunity to talk with her students about
issues of age and how age has become a powerful—and often invisible—mechanism
of social ordering in our society. Students discussed issues such as voting, driving
licenses, serving in the military, and drinking alcohol. In talking about the issue of
testing in school specifically, the students voiced their interest in having more say
in the curriculum—in what and how they were taught. This proved another important moment for Bethany to open space for the students to examine how they were
being positioned in society and the extent to which they had power to affect the
sanctioned influences (in this case, school) in their lives. Over these two days, they
also discussed adult perceptions of youth, wondering if the adults in schools—and
even those reporting the news—think youth are being disrespectful by protesting,

or as one student said, "adults just think the teenagers are just trying to get out of work."

Bethany also created a lesson for this week in which the students viewed a short documentary film made a few years prior by students at CHS in which the students investigated budgetary issues within the district. The film is replete with depictions of youth as smart, engaged, and concerned with broader sociopolitical issues. What became a fascinating discussion across both of these lessons involved not only depictions of youth in these texts (which were overwhelmingly positive), but also how some of the so-called adults in these texts were demeaning toward the youth within the texts. This point was perhaps best exemplified in the documentary when, in an interview with a group of students, the superintendent essentially dismissed their inquiry by saying that what they wanted to know about were "adult issues." By the end of this week, Bethany engaged students in opportunities for brainstorming possible media texts they might create to either critique damaging portrayals of youth in the media or provide more comprehensive or positive—or, as many of the students said, "more realistic"—representations of youth in the media.

Some Important Moves Bethany Made in This Unit

Curriculum is always in flux and being revised, particularly the first time through. This truism certainly holds for the unit discussed in this chapter. However, I want to highlight some particularly savvy moves Bethany made that could be useful for teachers considering similar unit plans.

- *Build on concepts and practices from previous coursework.* Having studied the concepts of rhetorical analysis and gender constructs earlier in the curriculum, Bethany leveraged these previously learned ideas to help students segue into the domain of analyzing media texts and thinking of youth and adolescence as social constructs. In this way, Bethany helped apprentice students into working with potentially unfamiliar concepts by scaffolding them with concepts more familiar to them.

- *Provide a heuristic for examining media but be open to students' modifications.* By no means are the key questions used in this unit the only way to analyze media texts, but having some type of heuristic for the students, at least to begin their analyses, proved to be an important component to the success of this unit. Bethany's use of key questions served as an anchor for the students. Yet her willingness to yield to students' own analytic approaches as they developed understandings of adolescence as a construct and the media's role in creating ideas of youth to modify and adapt to best meet the texts they were critiquing and their purposes for critiquing them was significant. From my vantage point, what was more valuable than the students being able to properly use the prescribed heuristic was their involvement in the more so-phisticated process of creating or extending it. In effect, Bethany positioned students as co-creators of the curriculum, which in some ways manifested the core ideas of this unit because it troubled typical relations between teacher, curriculum, and students.

- *Invite students to bring texts into the curriculum.* By far, the most engaged and animated moments in the curriculum were when students helped shape the content of it. Specifically, Bethany had students at different times bring in hard copies of media texts and other times contribute links and digital texts to the class Google Docs so all students could work with the catalog of texts. In addition to developing buy-in from students, this practice helped illuminate just how pervasive—and often "invisible" and taken for granted—these im-ages are in students' lives.

- *Examine the school's representations of youth.* Though this unit was focused on media texts, when Bethany had the students tour the school and photograph ways youth were being positioned within the institution, the students seemed to begin to make connections between the ideas they had been discussing in class related to the media, to something much more tangible in their lives. This move also had the effect of helping students think even more deeply about how ideas of youth have potential material effects or consequences on youth themselves.

- *Offer many different examples of positive portrayals of youth.* From my own experiences teaching critical media literacy, I worry that the negative and problematic representations in the media are highlighted to the point of pro-ducing an almost negative or defeated feeling in students. Therefore, what I appreciated about Bethany's approach was that she paid as much attention to more positive and comprehensive portrayals of youth in the media as she did to problematic and detrimental depictions. It is interesting—and tell-ing—to note that the former were more difficult to find, particularly within mainstream media. This balance seemed to give the students a sense of the problem but also a sense of potential solutions. Incidentally, these more posi-tive media texts also served as great mentor texts for many of the students' final projects.

Assessment: Revising Images of Youth in the Media

Throughout the unit, the students completed a wide range of formative assess-ments, including, for example, weekly reflections on what they were learning, short assignments in which they were required to connect what they were learn-ing in class with their observations in the media and school and other domains of their lives (e.g., sports, youth groups), participation in small- and whole-group discussions, and short analysis papers designed to help them use the heuristic for analyzing media texts for depictions of youth. The unit culminated in a summative project in which the students crafted a creative text that either critiqued media representations of youth or created alternative, asset-oriented images of youth in the media. For Bethany, it was extremely important that this unit position her students not only as consumers of media, but also, and in the spirit of the core ideas throughout the unit, as producers of media and culture. Figure 3.1 is the actual assignment Bethany gave to the students.

Final projects included short films, illustrations, comic strips, collages of media images, PowerPoint presentations, poetry, short fiction, as well as other textual modes. Students created both texts that critiqued dominant images of the media and texts that provided more positive, realistic media images. For example, one group of young men created a short film in which they satirized representations of teen boys as being destructive, aggressive, and hormonal. In the video, they set out

---

Figure 3.1. Bethany's assignment explaining the summative assessment.

Youth Representation in the Media

Assignment: Throughout this unit, we have explored representations of youth and adolescence/ts within various forms of media. Your task is to create a media text that critiques and/or represents youth more accurately/comprehensively. In other words, what is troubling about how youth and adolescence/ts is represented and how SHOULD youth and adolescence/ts be represented within our society?

Part One: The Actual Media Text

    Your task is to create a media text that either critiques or reconstructs the normative idea of adolescents/adolescence.

    Media Text Options
      1. Video
      2. Graphic Art
      3. Short Story
      4. Song/Music
      5. Cartoons/Graphics
      6. Webpage
      7. Other

    Requirements: Due to the variety of options/projects, requirements are difficult to pin down. I am looking for a solid presentation of effort and engagement as well as a thorough representation of your thoughts/knowledge on the subject of youth representations in the media.

Part Two: Meta-Analysis

    Requirements: 500-word essay that analyzes your final project. The goal of this piece is to explain what decisions you made and WHY you made them (think of the Key Questions for Media Literacy/Youth Representation). More details to come in class.

to show the stereotypes of teen boys and the reality of teen boys as they understood and experienced it. They set the video in school, since they thought this was an important setting in which these stereotypes get played out. One of the students involved in the project wrote the following in his meta-analysis of the project:

> We used the school as our setting for the video because it's a place where adults are in authoritative positions as well that it seems to be where teenage boy stereotypes seem to be put on the boys. We felt the school would be a good place to show that teenage boys do go to school, are polite to their friends, and take care of things.

In another project, a student created a PowerPoint presentation he delivered to his classmates about various representations of youth and teenagers in popular contemporary music. For example, he argues how much popular music (e.g., Jay Z's "Young Forever" and Katy Perry's "Last Friday Night") reveals teens to be troublemakers, involved in criminal activities, partiers, and irresponsible. He then contrasts these popular representations with a range of other, more positive representations of youth from the local community where they are involved in community service and committed and hardworking.

Interestingly, quite a few final projects focused not on youth but on adults. For instance, one project satirized adult anxieties about youth drug and alcohol use by drawing attention to the many states adopting marijuana laws. One of the main images in this project was an older man smiling while having a marijuana joint in his mouth and giving the thumbs up. The project provided statistical information about adult behavior involving alcohol and drugs. These projects, much like several of the discussions throughout the unit, illuminated how examining constructs of youth also calls into question the constructed nature of adults and adulthood—what is typically understood as the norm by which youth is judged as deviant or deficient. One of the points many students were trying to make in their final projects is that many behaviors attributed especially to youth are often behaviors of youth *and* adults.

Overall, these media texts demonstrated that the students were able to engage in the process of critiquing media representations of youth—calling out dominant, diminishing stereotypes—and create depictions that were more consonant with their understandings of youth in society. Bethany used two main criteria in evaluating these summative assessments. She was interested in the students' creativity with this project—that they took risks in their development of a final project. Particularly given the limited time they had, she was less interested in the projects being perfectly crafted and composed; rather, she wanted to see an authentic engagement with the ideas explored in the unit. Second, she was interested in the students' understanding of a critical perspective on teens and/or the category of youth. In this way, she wanted to make sure they developed an understanding of the relationships between youth as a social construct and the media's role in producing these ideas.

In addition to a creative text, Bethany had the students create a "meta-analysis" in which they had to explain the decision-making and rhetorical choices of their final projects. In this way, the assignment pushed the students to demonstrate their metacognitive awareness of rhetorical analysis as well as many of the concepts learned throughout the unit. It also functioned as a final way to have the students demonstrate their understanding of the heuristic learned and used throughout the unit, as they had to apply it to their own projects. Together, these two components of the final assessment revealed that the students had developed a keener sense of how the media worked to construct dominant images of youth in the media, and had developed skills to critique and create media texts.

Ideas for Trying This Out

Building on the strong work Bethany has begun, how might you develop your own curriculum that engages secondary students in an examination of representations of youth in the media? As you think of integrating this into your own teaching, it may be helpful to consider some of these ideas:

- *Delineations of representations of youth.* As we continue to think of innovative, engaging ways to build curriculum and work with secondary students around representations of youth in the media, it is imperative that we also think about how even the idea of youth and adolescence as social constructs needs to be further delineated by intersections with other social constructs and categories. For instance, how are rural youth depicted in the media? Urban youth? How do gender affiliations intersect with representations of youth in the media? What about youth who are immigrants in the United States? Youth from different countries? Different racial designations of youth? By broadening the scope of examining youth to include these other categories of representation, a critical media literacy will have much to say about the myriad experiences of young people, thus furthering the central premise of this book, to rethink naturalized and normative ideas of youth.

- *More reading of research-based texts on youth.* Though some research reading took place in this unit, my sense is that students would benefit greatly from reading social science research-based texts, histories of adolescence, and more mainstream texts that address ideas of adolescence as a construct (e.g., the *Huffington Post* articles). Chapter 2, for instance, provides an example of how explicitly reading and discussing these more scholarly and research-based texts works well in English classes when addressing ideas of adolescence and youth as cultural constructs.

- *Distributable texts.* Given time constraints and the newness of this particular iteration of this unit, Bethany was not able to generate with the students many venues for distribution of their final media text projects. As many literacy educators have demonstrated, having an authentic audience for whom students are preparing texts to distribute makes for richer literacy engagement. Therefore, in looking ahead, I would encourage teachers interested in this work to seek out ways for students to have actual audiences and venues for their final projects. With this topic, in particular, it seems imperative, given how rethinking ideas of youth and adolescence is part of a larger project of social critique and bringing about a more equitable world. (See Chapter 2 for examples of the effects of having a real audience in front of whom students could share their learning on adolescence, and see Chapter 5 for more ways to imagine assessment linked with advocacy and social justice.)

- *Move from ideas of youth to critical media literacy.* The way Bethany organized this particular unit is that ideas of the media were foregrounded and then discussions of youth and adolescence entered the curriculum. While I think this made good sense given this particular unit and group of students and previous curriculum, I also think it is worth experimenting with going in the opposite direction. Start with ideas of youth and adolescence and then move into thinking of the role the media plays in shaping these ideas. By foregrounding the concept rather than the medium or text set, this could allow for a more comprehensive examination of the topic of youth. In other words, emphasizing media first could potentially constrain the range of thinking and textual engagement that leading with the topic could broaden. In this way, the media portion of the unit would be a component of the broader aims of the unit.

- *Satire.* Many of these projects—particularly the one aimed at critiquing dominant, negative images—drew on satire. In retrospect, critiques of dominant views of youth are replete with satire, and so though we hadn't anticipated students' use of satire, in retrospect, it makes good sense. Therefore, in teaching a media unit focused on depictions of youth, you may be well prepared to expect aspects of satire to be employed by students. Therefore, it may make sense to position this unit after a unit on satire within the broader year-long curriculum so students can draw on this knowledge for this unit.

- *Deepening your own knowledge about adolescence and youth as cultural constructs.* Before embarking on a unit focused on media representations of youth, it seems a crucial first step to learn as much as you can about this topic. By now, my hope is that you've gleaned several entry points into these ideas. Embedded throughout this chapter, as well as in Chapter 1, and to come in subsequent chapters, are many texts, resources, and concepts to help you learn about how adolescence emerged as a category of representation, how it continues to circulate in our society as a seemingly naturalized stage of life, and how it constrains opportunities for youth.

- *Deepening your understanding of critical media literacy.* Throughout this chapter, I have offered several resources for becoming (more) familiar with the concepts related to critical media literacy. I want to reiterate that one particularly useful one is the Center for Media Literacy (www.medialit.org). Another great set of resources can be found at http://www.mediaed.org, which is the website for the nonprofit Media Education Foundation. This organization has a host of documentary films about media (and other topics) specifically designed for educators. As you deepen your thinking about teaching media literacy, I encourage you to consider the following items:

- *Set goals for engaging students with critical media literacy*. As you imagine creating a unit on media literacy, what are your goals? How might you—like Bethany or the work of the teachers in Ernest Morrell's book mentioned above (Morrell et al., 2013)—take into consideration your context (school, community, historical) and your larger curriculum to build a unit that makes sense for you and your students?

- *Ascertain what your students' past and current experiences are with media literacy*. Though they may not have had an opportunity to study it formally in an academic context, your students will have vast experiences with media and much to say about it. It could be very useful to take a stance of inquiry in trying to understand what your students' experiences and attitudes are toward media, as well as their interests for more formal study. In addition to just mindful teaching practices, this could be a good way to help re-position students as "experts" in the class related to curriculum. In many ways, what I am suggesting here is to re-position yourself as a "teacher-ethnographer" in which your job is to understand your students as consumers, producers, and distributors of media before you even begin the unit. This could also help you develop the goals for the unit I suggest in the bullet point above.

- *Inventory available technology and technical support*. Invariably, teaching a unit on media literacy will necessitate integrating a fair amount of technology into your teaching—even more so for the students' use than yours. Therefore, I suggest before beginning a unit on media, see what technology you have available in your school, how well it all works, and what support you have if devices break down. I also think it is important, as in the above point, to inventory your students' use of and skills with different technologies.

Closing Thoughts

Overwhelmingly, in their interviews the students talked about how much they enjoyed this unit. They specifically talked about it being unlike "regular English" and that it felt relevant to them in their lives. For Bethany, the unit was a huge success. She talked about increased motivation, as well as students' deepened sense of media—and more important for her, a better sense of how they interact with others in the world. I would like to end the chapter with her words from an email reflection she wrote to me that addressed her experiences of the unit:

> I read the rest of their [student] reflections, and a lot of students found a lot of value in the unit. They mentioned being more aware of media and the subtle messages contained therein. They also talked about being more aware of how they are perceived by others, but also how they sometimes judge others as well. That is huge to me. This unit helped them be more aware of the way they interact with people in society. . . . I call that a win!

The Teaching/s of Young Adult Literature: Using a Youth Lens to Analyze Adolescence in YAL

Sophia Tatiana Sarigianides, Robert Petrone, and Mark A. Lewis

Several years ago, Mark worked with a group of ninth-grade students who attended a predominantly white, middle-class, suburban high school. Their teachers, like many teachers across the country, chose to highlight young adult literature (YAL) in literature circles—hoping to increase their students' engagement with reading, among other social and curricular goals. Mark suggested *Monster* (2004) by Walter Dean Myers.

The novel follows the trial of Steve, who is accused of murder, but whose innocence or guilt remains ambiguous throughout the story, thereby opening up many avenues for student discussion on both his culpability and broader societal understandings of what it means to be guilty of a crime. The teachers were diligent in building appropriate instructional materials, including role sheets, reading logs, discussion prompts, and a closing essay asking the students to determine Steve's relative culpability. The students were engaged throughout the unit, often taking strong stands on Steve's innocence or guilt, his personal feelings, and what consequences he should endure.

Yet, when students submitted their essays, the content of the writing surprised Mark and the teachers. Despite the lively discussions in the students' literature circles and reading logs (discussions that rarely focused on ideas about connections between adolescence and race), a vast majority of the students revealed specific assumptions about Steve as an African American adolescent in their analyses. Namely, they based their decisions about his culpability on preconceived notions of the characteristics of youth of color in urban settings: They were all black criminals. Reading *Monster*, then, had the unintended consequence of reinforcing problematic, racist notions of urban, African American youth in this unit.

Reflecting on this experience now, perhaps Mark and the teachers should not have been so surprised that students' interpretations of Steve relied on racist stereotypes. The three of us, all of whom identify as white, understand as best we can from our positionalities the very complicated ways that racism functions systemically in the United States, insidiously affecting the ways that all Americans think and behave, consciously or not. And of course schools as institutions reflect systemic racism through the curriculum. For this reason, we are not interested in targeting any particular individuals or groups in the opening anecdote for racist readings of Steve Harmon in *Monster*.

Rather, and with the help of others who have considered these questions before us (see Groenke et al., 2015), this kind of experience has led the three of us to wonder about the messages YAL sends its readers about youth—especially youth of color and other minoritized youth—and to support teachers who aim to disrupt such stereotypical views through their curriculum.

As a body of writing that names its readership "young adults," YAL has much to say—and teach—about adolescence to the youth and the adults consuming it. In fact, YAL is by its very nature teaching ideas about youth, whether these lessons are explicit or implicit. As literary scholar Allison Waller explains, "fiction is as important as theory or science in creating our understanding of, and behaviour towards, young people" (Waller, 2010, p. 192). Following from ideas presented in Chapter 1, in which we discussed the ways that theory and science help create our understanding of and reactions toward young people, and Chapter 3, in which we focused on the role of the media in contributing to "beliefs" about youth, this chapter examines how YAL similarly participates in shaping our ideas about youth.

While YAL has an important place in the English language arts curriculum for many reasons, we believe that as English language arts teachers, we need to be mindful about how we use it in our classrooms with our students. As we've explored in previous chapters, our central concern involves the many messages found in YAL that rely on and reinforce diminished views of young people, which can lead to deficit-oriented ways of thinking about youth. For example, in the vignette that opens this chapter, Mark and the teachers he was working with overlooked how Steve might be viewed primarily as an urban youth of color, especially to their white students. As a class, they discussed with their students social constructions of race and how those constructions might negatively affect defendants. But they neglected to discuss with their students social constructions of adolescence, as well as the intersection of adolescence with race, in order to mitigate the possible preconceived notions they had about youth of color in urban settings and ascriptions of criminality to them. Ignoring the messages that many YA texts circulate about youth may lead to the development or perpetuation of instructional practices and policies that either stereotype youth, stereotype certain kinds of youth, or neglect to tap into the myriad ways youth are capable and able and exceed the expectations set up for them by society.

YAL inhabits a complicated terrain, with a wide variety of books with a wide variety of messages. At times, some YAL seems to promote stereotypes of youth; other times, YAL seems to critique these typical ways of thinking about young people and in doing so, offers alternatives for thinking about adolescence. Either way, we cannot approach YA texts uncritically regarding representations of youth. We believe it is important for English language arts teachers to interrogate—and to help your students to question—the lessons about young people that YAL teaches, and the ways YAL goes about teaching these lessons. Given these concerns, what might teachers who believe in the value of YAL do?

In this chapter, we ask: What does YAL teach about youth? And how can English language arts teachers who use YAL take up this question in their own instruction and selection of YAL? To do so, we present some specific readings of texts to demonstrate possibilities for analyzing YAL to focus on the messages the books are teaching about youth and adolescence. We anticipate that some of these readings might challenge your thinking about these particular texts and perhaps even the entire categorization of texts designated as YAL. Ultimately, our hope is that this approach helps you and your students view YAL in new ways that open conversations about how youth are represented through these and other YA texts and through society at large.

A Youth Lens with Young Adult Literature

We begin by identifying some specific YAL that either interrupts, calls attention to, or utilizes stereotyped ways of viewing youth. Using four YA texts, we employ a Youth Lens—the analytic approach we discussed in Chapter 2—to draw attention to a text's representations of adolescents as people and adolescence as a social category. The central question of a Youth Lens is: How do texts represent adolescents/ce? As we have stressed throughout this book, if you are familiar with other critical perspectives like a feminist, Marxist, or critical race theory lens, then you already understand part of how a Youth Lens works. For example, if a feminist lens works to expose gendered norms and stereotypes (i.e., how a particular text presents gender), a Youth Lens offers a way for readers to make visible the messages delivered explicitly and implicitly in a text about adolescence—whether or not that text openly controverts conventional ideas of adolescence. By offering students this critical tool, they can better take note of the many ways they are being defined by texts and thus learn to develop critical responses in relation to these characterizations.

We recognize that the type of analysis of YAL we are suggesting through a Youth Lens is a messy, nuanced process as YA texts sometimes challenge expectations of youth, sometimes reinforce common beliefs about adolescence, and sometimes do a bit of both. We also recognize that the type of analytic moves we are suggesting open up potential critiques of YAL that teachers and students may not have previously considered, especially given how celebrated YAL has been both in the public and within English education (e.g., YALSA's Celebrate Teen Literature Day every April; Herz & Gallo, 2005).

We understand this strange experience of feeling as though we have been reading and supporting texts unproblematically only to begin to notice that some of these texts rely on stereotypes of adolescence. This discomfort makes sense, and ultimately, is important to recognize. In fact, we suggest sharing this perspective with your students since it may reflect their own mixed reactions. Furthermore, making your own ambivalence visible might not only invite your students to grapple with their own but also position the students in your class as authorities on the topic of adolescence, especially in relation to the adults—here, teachers and authors—typically seen as authorities over youth. This discomfort may also engender entry points for the analysis of texts. Why are we uncomfortable rethinking adolescence as a social category and the myriad ways it challenges us to rethink our assumptions of youth? Our hope, then, is that the ideas we suggest in this chapter will actually facilitate more intellectually stimulating and pleasurable readings of YAL, as well as social justice–oriented perspectives for analyzing and teaching these books, perspectives that your students are likely going to take an enormous interest in given the focus on a social category that allegedly aptly describes them.

While impossible for us to cover the myriad lessons YAL teaches and the innumerable ways these books teach them, we want to model some ways that teachers can help students begin to see how YAL portrays youth. Even as we do so, we keep in mind our enthusiasm for YAL. As we and many other English educators and classroom teachers have seen, YAL often motivates youth to read, and it offers teachers exciting possibilities for making curricular connections with more canonical texts. Ultimately, though, like other texts, YA texts are not neutral in the political messages they send through their portrayals. And for the young people in your classrooms, the kinds of messages offered in YAL *for an audience named as "young adult"* matters greatly for any teacher committed to social justice aims since the portrayals sometimes found in such texts may reinforce dominant, problematic views of young people. In addition, for already marginalized youth, such depictions may actually be even more harmful in a body of writing allegedly representing "them."

In the upcoming section, we utilize a Youth Lens to focus on four key confident characterizations—or foundational beliefs—about adolescence, ideas that we introduced in Chapter 1. Identified by scholar Nancy Lesko (2012) to help bring attention to the fact that seemingly stable "truths" about youth can actually be traced to a specific, problematic history, these confident characterizations function to exemplify some of the key ways that youth are expected to behave, think, and function in society during the adolescent period. The four confident characterizations—or stereotypes—about youth include the following ideas:

1. youth can be signified by their specific age;
2. youth focus nearly exclusively on relations with their peers, rather than on relations with either younger children or adults;
3. youth are governed by their hormones; and
4. youth experience a slow coming-of-age into adulthood.

In the following analyses, we spend time on each of these confident characterizations. First, we discuss the way the confident characterization is commonly relied on or thought about culturally in the United States. Second, we share some critical views of the seemingly stable set of ideas about that confident characterization. Third, we provide examples from two YA texts that address that confident characterization in some way—reinforcing it, critiquing it, or doing some of both. Finally, we close each section with a set of general questions that this confident characterization might lead to that you could use on other texts featuring adolescence. It's also important to recognize that though in this chapter we draw on these four traits of adolescence identified by Lesko as entry points for analysis via a Youth Lens, there are many other ways to employ a Youth Lens. See the annotated bibliography for other examples of how we and others in English education have done so.

We focus all our discussion of YAL here on four texts to help illustrate the points we are trying to make. Benjamin Alire Sáenz's (2012) *Aristotle and Dante Discover the Secrets of the Universe* tells the story of how Aristotle and Dante, both Mexican American teens, find friendship and love for the first time amid complex family dynamics. Francesca Lia Block's (1989) *Weetzie Bat* tells the story of Weetzie and her experiences with sex, marriage, parenting, and love amid the backdrop of 1980s Los Angeles. Sherman Alexie's (2007) *The Absolutely True Diary of a*

Part-Time Indian chronicles the ninth-grade school year of Junior, the novel's protagonist, as he navigates leaving his American Indian reservation school district for the nearby white high school. As discussed briefly at the beginning of the chapter, Walter Dean Myers's (1999) *Monster*, through a blended genre text, tells the story of Steve Harmon, an African American young man who stands trial for murder.

Confident Characterization #1: Age

When it comes to ways of thinking about and knowing youth, virtually nothing trumps *age*. We are so steeped in age as a way of understanding youth, particularly people in their teen years, that it often functions as a way for adults to have immediate and often unexamined ideas about young people. It seems that once we know a youth's age, for instance, we often feel as though we know the person. "She's fifteen? Oh boy," you might hear—or even think. Nearly every age affiliated with the teen years has very particular associations.

This set of understandings makes sense to most of us since developmental theories of childhood and adolescence—with rigid, stage-based models of growth—dominate in teacher preparation programs and in parenting circles, as we discussed in Chapter 1. In other words, beginning from early childhood, parents and other adults are flooded with information about how specific ages come with specific milestones and behaviors (e.g., emotional, cognitive, physical). As a result, such views of young people—that we can understand much about who they are just by knowing their age—repeat in popular culture and in everyday thinking and exchanges.

Believing we understand something about youth simply because of their age functions as a common trope in US culture. In the words of Nancy Lesko, "age is a shorthand, a code that evokes what amounts to an 'epidemic of signification'" (2012, p. 4). By calling the "code" or "shorthand" of age an "epidemic of signification," Lesko exposes the weight given to age as something that tells us what to expect in youth and how to read what we see in youth's actions. Using the term *epidemic* to explain this idea to us, Lesko also designates this source of knowledge as problematic: Most of us see adolescents' age as a troubling period of time, and Lesko helps us to understand that *thinking* this way about youths' age is actually a bigger problem than the reality. Keeping in mind Lesko's critical stance, we suggest examining YAL for the lessons it teaches about the concept of age, including normative, age-based expectations.

In YAL, supplying characters' ages, particularly early on in a novel, is fairly commonplace. For instance, within a few pages of John Green's *Looking for Alaska* (2005), we know that Pudge, the main character, is sixteen; likewise, early in Alexie's *The Absolutely True Diary of a Part-Time Indian*, we learn that Junior is fourteen; and Katniss's age of sixteen is given to the reader within the first chapter of *The Hunger Games* (2008). This mention of age early in YAL texts is interesting in and of itself, but particularly when thinking of how much less commonplace this is in literary texts written for non-YA audiences.

Why this emphasis on age—and often, so immediately—in YAL? By referencing the protagonist's age early in YAL, writers find an expedient means of characterization. By telling us characters' ages, writers tap into deep cultural beliefs about what it means, for example, to be a "fifteen-year-old boy"—something that readers can take as self-evident and likely includes ideas about hormones, recklessness, and a lack of rationality—those characteristics we mentioned in Chapter 1 that arise when talking to people about what defines adolescents and adolescence. In this way, age—and the cultural assumptions surrounding age as a marker of identity—is used as a matter of fact. It is commonsense knowledge.

However, some texts draw attention to the cultural assumptions surrounding age in order to challenge those assumptions. For example, in Sáenz's 2012 award-winning novel, *Aristotle and Dante Discover the Secrets of the Universe*, the author directly confronts issues of age. Very early in the narrative, in a conversation with his mother, whom he loves and with whom he gets along, the adolescent protagonist, Ari, exposes key assumptions around age and adolescence/ts.

> "Maybe Richie Valens died young—but he did something. I mean, *he really did something*. Me? What have I done?"
>
> "You have time," she said. "There's plenty of time." The eternal optimist.
>
> *"Well, you have to become a person first,"* I said.
>
> She gave me a funny look.
>
> *"I'm fifteen."*
>
> "I know how old you are."
>
> *"Fifteen-year-olds don't qualify as people."*
>
> My mom laughed. She was a high school teacher. I knew she half agreed with me. (pp. 7–8; emphasis added)

Whereas age often goes unexamined in YAL, in *Aristotle and Dante*, Sáenz does something different. Sáenz references Ari's age only to immediately challenge the cultural beliefs that link particular ages to certain expectations of youth and adolescence. When Ari tell his mom, a high school teacher, that "fifteen-year-olds don't qualify as people," and that, before accomplishing anything significant, an adolescent has to "become a person first," he references the commonsense understanding that fifteen-year-olds—like other teens—are still incomplete, and "on their path" to adulthood, but not to be seen as individuals in their own right at the moment who are capable of taking on many difficult responsibilities and often withstand a lot.

And it is no accident that Ari chides his mom, a high school teacher, about these age-based beliefs. Such tenets about adolescence are reinforced in teacher education programs, most of which require courses in adolescent development that often leave such rigid, stage-based beliefs in developmental models of psychology unchallenged. Significantly, Ari's mom laughs at Ari's comment. Their easy relationship might be seen, in part, as a result of her ability to both laugh at Ari's critique of this stereotype of youth and the fact that she "half agreed" with the stereotype Ari was pointing to. In other words, she recognizes that she does somewhat hold on to such ideas at the same time that she is open to listening to how silly and unreasonable they are.

Sáenz coaches readers here to take note of this and other conventional views about youth—and Mexican Americans, and masculinity, and homosexuality—in this well-conceived novel, making it an effective text for students to explore. Teachers who use this book could guide students to consider this passage, asking questions like these: Are all fifteen-year-olds the same? What factors affect differences between fifteen-year-olds that you know? If some fifteen-year-olds share traits, do they also share them with youth—or adults—of a different age? Can we really know what to expect of specific youth just by knowing a generic age? (For additional ideas on how teachers might develop creative assessment designs tied to this and other confident characterizations, see Chapter 5.)

Whereas Sáenz references a specific age for his protagonist only to challenge what that age is supposed to signify to his readers, another way to critique expectations tied to youths' age is to leave out age markers altogether. This is exactly what Block does in her 1989 novella, *Weetzie Bat*. Set in Los Angeles and populated by fantastic elements like a genie and a witch, Weetzie and her three housemates live together, hang out all over kitschy L.A., decide to parent, and successfully do so despite many challenges. When we teach the book in English education courses, teachers in these courses want to know, "just how old is Weetzie, anyway?" Yet Block purposefully leaves out any references to age. We know that Weetzie and her best friend, Dirk, meet in art class in high school, but that is the only age-related reference in the novella. Besides Weetzie's pregnancy and the requisite nine-plus months expected of it, the novel excludes most references to time altogether. Without such references to age (and time), teachers may struggle with their responses to the plot and to characterization, especially when they imagine students in schools reading the novel.

As teachers, we can use these responses to raise important questions about *why*, as readers, we *need* to know Weetzie's age. What kind of information would age give us that would help our literary interpretation beyond the details shared with us? With this text and its matter-of-fact treatment of youth as sexual and desiring to parent and doing so effectively, answers to these questions might lead high school classes to notice how much our desire to know Weetzie's age is tied to very strong social admonitions about having sex "too early" and it leading to parenting "too early."

To be clear, we are not trying to promote sex in youth or to suggest that parenting is easy. But parenting isn't easy at any age, and youth are sexual whether their sexuality is condoned by adults or not. (There is much more to say about beliefs about sex, age, and even class and happiness, and we include references to further reading in the annotated bibliography for teachers interested in these questions and their representations in YAL.)

For our purposes here, however, this one example opens up a host of questions for teachers to raise with students: Do all books—and not just YAL—reference youths' age? When youths' ages are mentioned, what kinds of expectations are hitched to those references? Does the protagonist meet those expectations or not, and with what effects? When age references are not included, what effects does that create for you as a reader? Do you want to know a character's age? Why?

As you can surmise, we see age as an important potential entry point in trying to ascertain what YAL teaches about youth (and the adults claimed to be so different from them). Here are some additional questions to consider when reading YAL:

- Does the book reference the protagonist's or other youths' ages?
- Does the book refer to adults' ages or just those of youth?
- Does the book represent the character in ways that contradict your expectations of age?
- How does the text use age in characterization and plot development?
- Does the book use age to attach social expectations of youth—and adults—to that character? If so, to what effects?

As we have discussed above, exploring conceptions of age within YAL is important as it helps to reveal one of the most common ways youth are made sense of in our society. When we examine how age functions in texts and society as a guide for the way we think about—and sometimes judge—youth for their behavior, we can draw attention to whether the social expectations driving these judgments are apt, reasonable, and fair for the youth they constrain.

Confident Characterization #2: Peer-Orientations

Common wisdom about Western youth holds that teens prefer the company of peers to the company of adults, frequently avoiding the company of adults by choice. This belief in peer-orientation as a natural phenomenon also frequently identifies youth as being particularly susceptible to peer pressure, especially

pressure to engage in behaviors deemed reckless, irresponsible, and even dangerous. Of course, an understanding of peer-orientation relies on ideas tied to age:
"peers" are defined by age, especially when it comes to youth.

A historical view of adolescence offers us a critical vantage for understanding these ideas about youth and peer-orientation. According to Lesko (2012), one
preoccupation of the late nineteenth/early twentieth century that shaped ideas
about the new adolescent involved a *desire* to use peer groupings as a means for
reinforcing values that adults wanted youth to reflect and to uphold. Through
organizations like the Boy Scouts, for example, boys were expected to *coach each
other* toward values preidentified as estimable for individuals but also for the nation.
In other words, during the period when the new sciences (e.g., psychology) were
changing desires and expectations for adolescence, peer-orientation was *encouraged*
and *facilitated* by adults.

So, why care about peer-orientation as a historically "produced" idea that
now appears as something naturally linked with adolescence? By naturally ascrib-
ing peer-orientation to youth, we necessarily limit possibilities for (non-age-based)
relationships between youth and adults (and even younger children), and we
pathologize peer socialization when it does take place. For instance, in her classic study of seventh-grade girls' literacy lives, researcher Margaret Finders shows
how notions of peer-orientation differ quite dramatically between girls of different
socioeconomic backgrounds. Whereas middle-class girls, she found, desired strict,
age-based peer relations (and had them reinforced by the adults in their lives with
the same expectations), the working class girls in her study preferred the company
of adults to their age-based peers. Unfortunately, for the working-class girls, their
teachers and the school writ large—also operating from the same "commonsense"
belief that teen girls wanted to distance themselves from adults and preferred to
gravitate toward their peers—actually pulled away from their relationships with
these girls and doing so put the girls at a social and academic disadvantage. Thus,
the idea that youths naturally desire peer-orientation is not only false or not a
"natural" expectation, but it is limiting for youth not culturally privileged by this
expectation.

Therefore, we suggest examining YAL for the lessons it teaches about
the concept of peer-orientation and notions of "proper" or "appropriate" social
relations for youth. One way that teachers can help their students question and
challenge ideas about youths' peer-orientation is to explore how YAL depicts such
social relations. In some books, peer-orientation is depicted unproblematically; in
other texts, peer-orientation is critiqued; in most YAL it is represented somewhere
in between. For us, the important point to make regarding the "confident characterization" of peer-orientation as an entry point into analysis of YAL is that it can

be used to help teachers and students expose the construct of adolescence and think more critically about the ways texts position youth as participants in the world. In this way, this approach helps us talk with our students about the various stereotypes aimed at them and the ways these align or don't with their lived experiences and ways of making sense of their own lives and social relations.

In Block's *Weetzie Bat*, for example, the four main characters seem to uphold expectations of peer-orientation. Weetzie, Dirk, Duck, and My Secret Agent Lover Man spend most of their time hanging out with each other at the beach, in their shared home, making films, and driving around Los Angeles. They seem to epitomize a Western adolescence of peer-based social relations dominating their time, interest, and attention. But a closer look at the text reveals that they also elect to spend time with Jah-Love and Ping Chong and their baby. Though, as we mentioned above, none of the characters are given ages, Jah-Love and Ping Chong meet in Jamaica and have jobs there and so seem to be older than Weetzie and her group, though, again, we ultimately don't know anyone's specific age. But Weetzie also enjoys and seeks out time with each of her divorced parents. For example, she dines with Charlie Bat, her dad, when he visits from New York City, and visits him on the East Coast as well. And before seeing Weetzie spend time with her parents, we saw her and Dirk seek out the company of Grandma Fifi, Dirk's grandmother, for life advice and to enjoy her collection of "vintage" clothing. So, while these young people do spend much of their time together, they also want to and do spend time with the adults in their lives, both those related to them and others who are pure social connections.

What is particularly significant in *Weetzie Bat* is how "normal" or matter-of-fact it is for these youth characters to spend time with both other youth and/or adults. In the novel, neither set of relations is pathologized or seen as unusual or problematic for the characters. However, based on our experiences teaching this text, the relations between youth and adults often cause dissonance for readers since the text disrupts normative expectations for such relationships. In this way, the novel delivers unconventional presentations of adolescent-adult relations without fanfare. By presenting these diverse relationships as normative, the novel offers teachers and students an excellent entry point to interrogate societal expectations for peer-orientation and the ways they constrain or open up ways of being in relation to different groups of people (e.g., adults, youth, children).

Another way that YAL draws attention to conventions about youth might be more explicit. In Sáenz's *Aristotle and Dante*, for example, Ari observes the easy relationship that his best friend, Dante, enjoys with both of his parents. Discussing the possibility of ever running away from home, Dante says he would never do it. Ari follows Dante's response with a question:

"Why not?"

"You want me to tell you a secret?"

"Sure."

"I'm crazy about my mom and dad."

That really made me smile. I'd never heard anyone say that about their parents. I mean, no one was crazy about their parents. Except Dante. (Sáenz, 2012, p. 21)

Though Sáenz does not show the boys socializing with adults outside the family, he does characterize Dante, especially, as eager to spend time with his father and mother, calling readers' attention to this trait as unusual. Sáenz reinforces this point in the first scene when Ari visits Dante's home. Dante walks in and goes straight to his father to kiss him. Ari comments immediately: "I would never have done that. Not ever" (p. 24). Ari notes that sometimes his exchanges with his mother are easy and "uncomplicated" like those he witnesses between Dante and his father; but never with his own father, a relationship that is one of the key foci of this complex novel. Yet, even in this depiction of a son not spending time with his father, in Sáenz's text, it is a *problem* for the protagonist and one that preoccupies him, rather than a norm that readers are to expect of youth who "naturally" recoil from their parents for the preferred option of being with peers.

Yes, Ari and Dante enjoy their time together tremendously, especially since they are each other's first-ever closest friend, and later, first love. But this depiction is one part of a complex rendering of their desires and preoccupations that also features numerous scenes observing, enjoying, and spending time with their parents. This is particularly remarkable in young adult literature given that so much of the literature characterized as such involves dead or otherwise absent parents. Imagining teens as anything but peer-focused and distancing themselves from their parents strikes many of us as highly unusual. For some youth taking up such norms, these social expectations may become sources of pressure onto peers to avoid—or deny—strong, healthy relations with adults. Yet perhaps these views are merely ones we have inherited from *desires* generated at the turn of the previous century and solidified through film and writing.

More than even age, we see an emphasis on peer-orientation and social relations within YAL as offering teachers and students great potential for not only engaging texts but for rethinking—and reconfiguring—social relations in society, particularly between youth and adults. Youth are so easily and quickly relegated to only caring about and being preoccupied by their age-based peer relationships that other types of relationships become unknowable or even impossible. In other words, this expectation limits both adults' and youths' ability to engage in productive, nonadversarial relationships with one another. How many times have we—and perhaps you, too—heard adults lamenting at how teenagers want nothing to do with them or any adults? And yet, in some of our own research, as well as the research of others, it is with adults that youth often desire to build solid relationships.

This focus on peer and social relationships is particularly generative for teachers to discuss with their students by asking: How do you—students—see peer-orientation in your life? Do you follow these social expectations of Western youth? Imagine discussions with students analyzing the relationships in YAL (and even pop culture) between teachers and students—and how schools themselves help to produce these relations.

Guiding students to think about the expectation of peer-orientation in youth, teachers might pose some of the following questions for students reading YAL:

- How does the book depict a character's desire to socialize?

- Do youth in the book desire to socialize with peers only, or also with adults?

- How is peer pressure depicted? Do youth try potentially problematic behaviors because of pressure to do so from others, or for other reasons like curiosity?

- Do characters' desires for socialization depend on differences in cultural background? In other words, do characters from various cultural backgrounds show conventional views about peer-orientation or different ones?

As with expectations tied to a youth's specific age, guiding students to think and respond to expectations about peer-orientation can be a fruitful and exciting way to help students more deeply engage these literary texts as well as examine the myriad ways broader society relies on and/or pushes against so-called normal social relations for youth. As demonstrated in Chapter 2, where Rachel has her students read *The Catcher in the Rye* through a Youth Lens, this type of work has the power to affect not only the ways students read but also how they participate in the world.

Confident Characterization #3: Hormones

Both through scholarly sources and popular dialogue, adolescents are regularly thought about in terms of the surge of hormones that brings bodily changes and seemingly difficult-to-control urges. As we have talked about in earlier chapters, adult authorities often describe adolescents as less rational as a result of incomplete development of the prefrontal cortex, and as hyper-emotional as a result of fluxes in hormonal surges. Ultimately, youth—like middle-aged women experiencing different hormonal shifts—are viewed as being passively governed by the body.

Ways of talking about youth in contemporary society, particularly through the lens of developmental psychology and biology, are increasingly rooted in the body—captured in phrases such as "raging hormones" and the "teenage brain."

These renderings of adolescence and youth position the experiences of teenagers as being inherent in their bodies and minds and not influenced much by their circumstances—whether those circumstances connect to demographics like class, race, or gender; or place, like rural, urban, suburban; or other sociocultural factors that shape people's lives in powerful ways, like choices tied to one's religious beliefs, or responsibilities like child-rearing or jobs.

Because typical ways of understanding youth ignore the sociocultural features that affect changes happening in their bodies, we recommend that teachers help youth examine depictions of adolescent characters' responses to such bodily urges in YAL. In other words, how does YAL depict the ways that youth respond to the body's influences? Of course, some books rely on these stereotypes of raging hormones, whereas other texts critique them. Regardless, there are implicit and explicit messages about youth in relation to biology being "taught" in all of these texts. Our purpose in this section is to help you think about the lessons taught about and to youth surrounding notions of biology. Our hope is that by examining YAL through this entry point, you might open up dialogue with students about the veracity of such ideas in our society. As seen in Chapter 3, the high school students studying media depictions of youth had much to say regarding how youth were being depicted as mostly governed by their "teenage brains." Therefore, we suggest similarly examining YAL for the lessons it teaches about the concept of the body in relation to youth characters.

Junior, in Alexie's *The Absolutely True Diary of a Part-Time Indian*, seems to perfectly match the stereotyped depiction of an adolescent boy. Soon after he introduces himself to us, he shares his unabashed love of masturbation and insists that it is natural and that everyone does it. Yet, in the same chapter and in relation to this response to hormones, he also shares the way that geometry affects him hormonally too.

> I was fourteen and it was my first day of high school. I was happy about that. And I was most especially excited about my first geometry class.
>
> Yep, I have to admit that isosceles triangles make me feel *hormonal*. (p. 25, emphasis in original).

Once he explains his "normal" love of masturbation as a reaction to hormones, and his heteronormative appreciation of women and their curves, he returns to his love of math. "But, the thing is, no matter how much time my thumbs and I spend with the curves of imaginary women, I am much more in love with the right angles of buildings" (p. 26). Alexie plays here with adolescent drives governed by the body and redirects them to Junior's interest in math. We see this as light play; Alexie is not drawing attention to this social construct in order to critique it, like Sáenz does with age. Rather, Alexie draws on preexisting expectations of youth and uses them to help him twist his characterization of a "normal" adolescent boy to also include a love of math, something we might not expect.

Alexie uses this same expectation of a sexual, hormonal adolescence later in the book in an exchange between Junior and his new friend in the town of Reardan, Gordy, the smartest boy in the school. Gordy helps Junior learn how to read like a serious student, but he also emphasizes the need for joy and pleasure in doing something one loves well, not taking it too seriously. He explains his idea to Junior by describing Junior's love of drawing as something that gives him a "boner." When Gordy realizes that Junior may be taking his language too literally, Gordy clarifies.

> "Well, I don't mean boner in the sexual sense," Gordy said. "I don't think you should run through life with a real erect penis. But you should approach each book—you should approach life—with the real possibility that you might get a metaphorical boner at any point."
>
> "A metaphorical boner!" I shouted. "What the heck is a metaphorical boner?"
> Gordy laughed.
> "When I say boner, I really mean joy," he said.
> "Then why didn't you say joy? You didn't have to say boner. Whenever I think about boners, I get confused."
> "Boner is funnier. And more joyful." (pp. 97–98).

Obviously, there is shock value—and comic relief—in including a rather lengthy discussion of erections in the midst of a book focused on the suffering that comes from being a poor, reservation American Indian with few opportunities. Yet Alexie's turn to adolescent boys' erections to discuss the joy of dedicating oneself wholly to something one loves relies on a commonplace, a shorthand, when it comes to thinking about adolescence, and adolescent masculinity especially. As with Junior's expressed "hormonal" feelings about isosceles triangles to show his love of geometry, here Gordy identifies the pleasures that accompany serious study and ambition through hormonal erections. We expect high school boys to be governed by hormones that direct their actions toward their sexual desires, yet here, these drives are directed to the pursuit of learning and the discipline of art. Again, we do not see Alexie critiquing dominant discourses of adolescence through these metaphors the way that we have shown other authors doing. Instead, he relies on them for characterization that he redirects toward layered views of these two young men.

In contrast, Block's *Weetzie Bat* takes a different approach to the commonplace of "raging hormones" in characterizing young people. Rather than draw exaggerated attention to youths' sexuality, in Block's novella, young people's sexuality is rendered as a matter of fact: Youth are sexual. It is not treated as a big deal, or as something that deserves social condemnation. Weetzie and her housemates have sex, and even desire to parent and go about getting pregnant very deliberately. In fact, the scene that (may) be the occasion of Weetzie's conception of Cherokee, her first daughter, helps readers see how Block treats "raging hormones." Whereas most adults would imagine that young people getting pregnant and parenting would be the result of out-of-control hormones, quite the opposite is the case in this novella. Once My Secret Agent Lover Man refuses to parent with Weetzie, their housemates, Dirk and Duck, who are partners and her best friends, approach her with a plan to help her get pregnant and to participate in raising the child together as a multiparent family.

One might expect the scene that describes this event to be graphic; instead, the scene is awkward and comical. "Weetzie changed into her lace negligée from Trashy Lingerie and went into Dirk and Duck's room and climbed into bed between Dirk and Duck. They all just sat there, bolt upright, listening to 'I Wanna Hold Your Hand'" (Block, 1989, pp. 57–58). The three housemates are uncomfortable about the situation, so they play the Beatles' song "I Wanna Hold Your Hand" and the song title takes the place of any descriptions of the sex act itself. The group is hardly taken over by raging hormones; they have a purpose, and one for which they all got tested for STDs before engaging in the act that comes off as more rational than reckless. As with age and peer-orientation, Block can be seen to challenge confident characterizations of youth by delivering shifts in adolescent behaviors without fanfare as a potential new norm.

More than age and peer/social relations, an emphasis on the body and sexuality within YAL has the potential to spark the most provocative and exciting possibilities for the classroom. How do secondary-age students make sense of the broader discourses of how their bodies and minds govern not only their behavior but also how they are taught, administered, disciplined, and so on? How do depictions in YAL help them make sense of these things? This line of inquiry can open up so many possibilities for students and teachers to interrogate not only YA texts but also school and public/community policies related to issues such as dress codes, banned books, and censorship. Second only to violence, so many YAL books (including Alexie's) are banned from schools due to their sexual content. Can you imagine working with students to examine some of these instances to understand what assumptions about youth and their bodies underlie many of these decisions? Dress code policies within secondary schools have continued to make national headlines in recent years and could also provide an interesting way to help move students toward such literary analyses—especially of YAL—to read the "world" as well. (See, for example, a recent instance from Helena High School in Montana of a "no bra" movement among students at the school as a form of protest to the sexist dress code policies [Free, 2016].)

Some additional questions to consider when guiding your students to analyze portrayals of youth as governed by their bodies or "hormonal" include:

- Does the book characterize the protagonist as full of "raging hormones"?
- How do peers or the adults around these characters discuss the teenage body as shaping youths' behaviors around sex or their emotional reactions?
- Are characters who abstain from acting on their raging hormones seen as normal youth?
- How do ideas about teenagers' bodies and minds shape the characters, plot, and even reader expectations and surprises in the text?
- Are extenuating circumstances and factors (e.g., religion, lack of interest in sex) given weight in developing characterization around sex?
- If characters are depicted as sexually active, how does the narrative regard their sexuality? In other words, do other characters or the narrative voice judge them or treat it as a matter of fact?

We also suggest this: The topic of youth and sexuality may seem not only sensitive to discuss in school settings, but even uncomfortable for you. If so, please see the annotated bibliography for suggested additional reading that might help you delve more deeply into the topic of youths' sexuality.

Confident Characterization #4: Coming of Age

Young people—and literature that features youth or is directed at youth—often are described as "coming of age." Part of what is signaled by the phrase "coming of age" is that youth are not yet what they are supposed to become: adults. Therefore, they are seen as being "in transition," "still becoming" what they are supposed to eventually be. Additionally, this coming of age is often understood as having a "proper" unfurling—designated by a slowness to its temporality. Young people are regularly depicted as focused more on themselves than the real world, apart from difficult life concerns. These normative conceptions and expectations of coming of age are often marked, too, by rituals and cultural events (e.g., the high school prom) designed to help signal different moments along this "proper" trajectory.

As we discussed in Chapter 1, though, this coming of age characterization of adolescence emerged more as a way of monitoring, regulating, and administering the newly created category of people known as "adolescents" than it is connected to any sense of inevitability that is biologically driven. In fact, in many instances, the typical coming of age prescribed for youth is not available for many young people shut out of its expectations because of class-based constraints. For poor and some middle-class youth, holding down a job may be an expectation to help their family survive or thrive. Not having the superfluous cash for typical "leisure" activities that involve spending precludes many young people from this "natural" expectation. In other words, a leisurely, slow coming of age is both socially constructed and marginalizing for many young people. Therefore, we suggest examining YAL for the lessons it teaches about the concept of coming of age and notions of "proper" or "appropriate" in terms of development.

One of the ways to examine how YAL portrays the idea of youth coming of age into adulthood is to compare and contrast how youth are portrayed in relation to adults or "adult" responsibilities or traits. Because adolescence is defined in relation to "adulthood" (i.e., adolescents are considered to be "in transition" to the destination of adulthood rather than seen as being who they are within the moment), its definition pitches the two categories as being opposed, so we might expect youth to reflect traits or to have experiences that are different from those of "adults."

In *The Absolutely True Diary of a Part-Time Indian*, Sherman Alexie describes Junior, the protagonist, as fourteen, best friends with Rowdy, who protects him from bullies on the reservation, and with whom he shares a love of basketball. These traits suggest a conventional portrayal of adolescence, especially when compared with Junior's candor about loving to masturbate. Yet, in the climactic scene of the basketball rematch between the mostly white Reardan team on which Junior plays and the solely American Indian Wellpinit reservation team on which Rowdy plays, Alexie makes sure to point out enormous differences between the members of the two teams.

Junior's mostly white, middle-class team has just beaten Rowdy's Wellpinit team, and Alexie raises the energy of the narrative for readers to cheer for Junior as the underdog because he had been physically injured by his own reservation team the first time they played together: They saw him as a white-loving traitor. "We had defeated the enemy! We had defeated the champions! We were David who'd thrown a stone into the brain of Goliath!" (p. 196). Yet, immediately after this elation, Junior, following his father's gaze in the stands, also looks over at the Wellpinit team and begins to make new realizations. "I realized that my team, the Reardan Indians, was Goliath" (p. 196). Here, Junior begins to list the many ways that the Wellpinit players carried different and heavier burdens than the middle-class, white Reardan players. For example, in relation to the white Reardan players, *all* of whom were going to college; drove their own cars; had iPods and cellphones and multiple options for clothing to wear to school; and had parents with "good jobs," the Wellpinit reservation team played under very different circumstances. Junior describes his former teammates as unlikely to have all had breakfast that day. Additionally, he knew of many specific players with parents who were either alcoholics, drug dealers, or in prison. Finally, he realizes, "I knew that none of them were going to college. Not one of them" (p. 197). Junior concludes, "Okay, so maybe my white teammates had problems, serious problems, but none of their problems was life threatening" (p. 197).

Though Junior elects to leave his reservation school to attend the white middle-class school twenty-three miles from his home, and though he develops a crush on Penelope whom he sort of dates, and attends the prom, and even gets invited to a post-dance gathering with friends at a local eatery, ultimately, Junior's problems are bigger than concerns solely tied to such "coming of age" experiences as dating and socializing. Junior's problems and preoccupations—like those of his reservation peers—center on issues tied to his poverty and race and the history of oppression suffered by American Indians at the hands of whites in the United States. Race and class supersede "adolescence" when it comes to the specific coming of age experiences expected of youth. Of course, Junior, like his white peers, is growing up, having new experiences, learning more, and maturing. But his adolescence is not one protected from "adult" concerns like the adolescence available to his white Reardan peers and marked by such events as "the big game" and "prom." His adolescence cannot involve a "slow" transition to an adulthood that is different from what he experiences as a youth; in Junior's view, without making the drastic and unpopular and scary decision to leave the reservation to attend a white school— even a nonaffluent white school populated by rural kids—Junior's adulthood, like his youth, will remain constrained by poverty and the suffering connected to it.

Readers can think about these representations of coming of age as a non-white, poor adolescent in another way. If adolescence is a period of future-oriented thinking and imagining—focusing on the adulthood to come rather than what is going on now just for itself—and if ideas poured into the shape of adolescence included as much hope as worry at the turn of the prior century, then searching for the hopefulness in adolescent portrayals is part of examining this social category. And yet, very overtly, Junior engages in a conversation with his father about the place of hope in their world.

> "Who has the most hope?" I asked.
> Mom and Dad looked at each other. They studied each other's eyes, you know, like they had antennas and were sending radio signals to each other. And then they both looked back at me.
> "Come on," I said. "Who has the most hope?"
> "White people," my parents said at the same time. (p. 45)

Their response affirmed Junior's perception and helped to solidify his decision to leave the reservation school and begin attending the white school in Reardan. Yet this analysis of hope continues when he arrives at the school and studies the confidence, relative wealth, and opportunities the students have at a white school just twenty-three miles away. In fact, Alexie complements the narrative treatment of hope with a full-page image contrasting a white male adolescence and American Indian male adolescence in terms of hope. In contrast to the American Indian youth's "vanishing past," and "bone-crushing reality" [of rampant alcoholism and poverty], white male adolescence is characterized by "a bright future," "positive role models," and, plainly, "hope" (p. 57). One could argue that the youth experienced on the reservation differs little from the experiences available to adults: Those living on the reservation have little to hope for in terms of change and better lives. All the hope they identify is tied to the lives of white people.

There is more to unpack here, and much more that teachers can read to prepare for a complex discussion around race and class differences. But adding into the discussion an examination of the meanings and possibilities attached to an *adolescence* that is poor and nonwhite exposes the ways that the entire category of adolescence is raced as white and classed as middle class, as we discussed in Chapter 1. Many of the expectations attached to adolescence against which adults and other youth hold young people in and out of school come from expectations mapped onto white, middle-class youth, leaving out a large swath of young people precluded from its possibilities. In some cases, even the diminished category of adolescence is a coveted and unattainable category.

Another way to explore the expectation of a slow coming of age in YAL is to note what happens when youth characters violate the "proper" path to adulthood in these narratives. As we discussed in Chapter 1, adolescents are expected to follow "ordered" paths to adulthood that push off too many responsibilities, focus on peer relations, and refrain from sex with an implicit promise that if all the "steps" are followed correctly, a (happy) and successful adulthood follows. There are many ways for young adult characters to break from this proper trajectory to adulthood: precocious sexuality, pregnancy, child-rearing, excessive violence, and criminality are some examples.

In Myers's award-winning *Monster*, readers meet Steve Harmon, an African American high school age youth, after he has already been arrested for his alleged participation in a robbery that resulted in the murder of a shopkeeper. The narrative comprises a multimodal story that includes a screenplay Steve is writing to tell his story while experiencing it in jail; a journal he keeps; grainy, black-and-white photographs that blur his features as they focus on cell bars and images reminiscent of security cameras; and courtroom drawings. Part of the strategy utilized by the prosecution involves connecting Steve to the legally adult coparticipants in the crime whom his defense attorney explains are people that the jury will not trust.

Scholars in English education have pointed out that, very often, white teachers hold to beliefs that view youth of color through deficit lenses. Writing in a 2015 special issue of *English Journal* focused on rethinking English teaching by rethinking adolescence, several scholars who prepare mostly white English teacher candidates discussed the ways that teacher candidates' views about youth of color are based on the kind of white, middle-class adolescence they experienced themselves (Groenke et al., 2015). In the excerpt that follows, teacher educators Wendy Glenn and Chonika Coleman-King converse about this topic:

Wendy: When my students talk about male teens of color (in the context of the novels we read and discuss), they often hold two seemingly opposing perspectives—*"these kids have to grow up so fast because of their difficult circumstances"* and "these kids don't have the support systems that help them grow up successfully."

Chonika: And that they aren't loved. In a text like *Monster* the beginning teachers don't focus on the love and support of the family, they focus on the pieces that reinforce stereotypes. . . . One theme I see across adolescence for youth of color is that they take on more adult responsibilities, but to our students that does not seem like adolescence because it's not their version of adolescence. (p. 37, emphasis added)

With Steve Harmon in *Monster*, readers can very easily slip into seeing Steve as a stereotyped African American male youth who is excessively violent, especially if they focus on the mode of the narrative that features the grainy photographic images. For example, though Steve portrays his vulnerabilities as a kid terrified of what he sees and hears in the jail populated by adults, in the grainy photographs, he is mostly shot out of focus, or in the background, with the image focusing more on the cell bars in the foreground, for example, emphasizing where he is now rather than who he is as a person. In fact, readers in Sophia's classes have talked about how the security images of Steve in the store remind them of similar images in the news when a security tape seemingly captures a criminal in the act. Significantly, we see Steve from a distance in these images, without internal monologue to complement stock images populating the media. Here, as in the screenplay scenes in the courtroom, Steve and his defense attorney fight conventional scripts about African American youth caught up in dangerous, criminal acts. These scripts neglect information that counters such stereotypes, like the fact that he comes from a loving, supportive family and attends a magnet public New York City high school like Stuyvesant for which he had to test in to be accepted.

To bring us back to the expectation of a slow coming of age for adolescence, youth of color caught in the criminal justice system—like youth who get pregnant or parent "too early"—tend to be thrust out of the category of "adolescence" because they "have to grow up so fast because of their difficult circumstances." They are already engaged in behavior and activities reserved for "adults." In Myers's hands, with the self-proclaimed aim of making sure that readers see youth of color as "human" (see Myers's 2014 op-ed in the *New York Times*, "Where Are All the People of Color in Children's Books?"), juxtaposing stories and images of Steve through multiple modes invites readers to consider how the character might appear different—both in terms of his culpability around the crime, but also as an adolescent—when we see him through different narrative modes that feature a different story of who he is.

Calling attention to these complex versions of Steve as an African American male youth caught in the criminal justice system, and of Junior, a reservation American Indian contrasting his "bone crushing reality" to the hopefulness attached to white, middle-class youth, will help your students consider to what extent the entire category of adolescence is raced and classed—and socially constructed. Some additional questions that could drive an inquiry into portrayals of coming of age might include:

- Is the protagonist afforded the "luxury" of a slow, leisurely coming of age? If not, does the character want one? Why not? If not, is the character marked as not normal?

- Is the success—or happiness—of the character dependent on a "normal" coming of age? What does that normal coming of age involve?

- What types of responsibilities do youth characters hold/carry? Are they, for instance, contributing to the household economy? Helping to raise their younger siblings? Do these responsibilities interfere with or preclude a "normal" coming of age, or do the characters take it for granted that these are their responsibilities?

An emphasis on "coming of age" exposes adolescence as a sociocultural construct and anything but a universal experience. More important, though, it reveals how the construct (similar to the example above related to peer-orientation and social class) inherently advantages certain youth and disadvantages other youth along lines of race and class. This is why it is important—crucial, really—to examine the various stereotypes and confident characterizations of youth often circulating through YAL with the students in your classes, who may take such portrayals as reinforcement of how they—and other youth—are expected to be.

Closing Thoughts

As we mentioned at the beginning of this chapter, it is vital that teachers and teacher educators read YAL more critically, particularly for the messages the stories communicate about young people. By offering these four entry points from a Youth Lens perspective, we hope to have provided a way for readers of YAL to examine whether a story reifies or disrupts commonsensical, stereotypical ideas and understandings of youth and adolescence. Essentially, we urge teachers to ask whose adolescence is being represented in YAL, and then encourage their middle and high school students to challenge and critique any representations that rely on stereotypes, particularly those that unfairly portray youth.

From these entry points for literary analysis, we also hope in this chapter to offer pedagogical entry points, so to speak. Specifically, as we suggest in a few places throughout the chapter, our aim is to provide a way (which will be expanded in the next chapter) to think about teaching YAL that not only helps students open up interpretive possibilities as they relate to representations of youth and adolescence within the texts, but also to think about how these ideas of youth circulate in society and can be rethought and reconfigured for more equitable possibilities for actual youth in your classes picking up these texts. To borrow from critical literacy scholarship, our aim is to help teachers teach YAL to help students read the "word and the world"—in this instance, the world being how youth and adolescence are understood, advocated for, and administered in our society. For example, as discussed above, a focus on the confident characterization of raging hormones can help students to interrogate policies that govern the clothing that is and is not permissible for them within schools. Similarly, they can examine the types of reasoning about youth used in cases of censored books. Regarding coming of age, teachers can use YAL to help students examine the myriad ways ideas of "adolescence" are delineated by race and class and how the very concept of adolescence inherently marginalizes and privileges different groups of youth—all the while attempting to push these differences away by positioning adolescence as a universal experience more or less out of reach of sociocultural factors. Finally, as explored above, teachers can use the confident characterization related to peer-orientation to help students examine how institutions such as schools as well as popular culture reify and make difficult amenable, productive relationships across age groups. In these and other ways, more of which will be explored in the next chapter, teaching YAL through a Youth Lens opens up possibilities for teachers to enact a pedagogy aligned with social justice aims focused on the youth in their classes.

Chapter Five

Implications for Assessment: Project Ideas for Featuring Adolescence in English Class

Sophia Tatiana Sarigianides, Robert Petrone, and Mark A. Lewis

While presenting at Sophia's university to an audience of mostly preservice teachers, but also professors and experienced local teachers, Nicole, a high school senior, shared what she learned about teacher thinking on adolescence within a unit on *The Catcher in the Rye* (1951) in her AP English class. To open her presentation, Nicole cited a professor in the field of English education, Margaret Finders, to explain how teachers stereotype youth in problematic ways.

> Teachers expect adolescents to be out of control and full of raging hormones. Finders explains this mindset: "You take a nice kid, and then puberty kicks in, and the kid becomes nothing but a bundle of raging hormones." When teachers walk into a classroom, they expect students to be wild, out of control, full of hormones, hard-headed, stubborn, causing extreme disruption, and having no sense of direction. Teachers expect these things, yet, teachers complain when students live up to these expectations. Teachers expect one thing, but want another.

In this assessment that fell near the end of a unit focused on examining representations of adolescents in literature—especially Holden Caulfield's portrayal as an
adolescent male, discussed in Chapter 2—Nicole and her classmates were required
to shape and deliver a presentation to a university audience. Their presentations
focused on what they learned about adolescence as a social construct, what they
learned about teachers' ideas of adolescence, and how they applied this learning to
literary analysis and to their lives. They were told that the audience mainly included future English teachers, so that their ideas might have an impact on future
middle and high school students like themselves.

   This assessment terrified the students from the beginning of the semester,
and especially this fall evening on Sophia's university campus. The audience to
whom the black and Latinx students were speaking included about fifty adults,
all teachers at one level of preparation or experience or another, nearly all white.
Nicole's presentation closed with her ideas of the implications of teacher's beliefs
about adolescence, all drawing from her reading of research on teacher thinking about adolescence by scholar Margaret Finders: "When teachers come into
a classroom expecting such behavior from students, they spend their class time
disciplining students, molding them into what they want them to be, and less
time teaching." After Nicole and her classmates finished their presentations, the
students on stage joined the college students and other adults in the audience in
break-out groups. Now the high school seniors were interacting as participants—
but really, as participant-experts—with university students and local teachers,
working together to analyze a short story, Jamaica Kincaid's (1978) "Girl," for its
representations of adolescence.

   As Sophia moved around the room to check in with each group, one of her
university students called her over. The preservice teacher had just finished her
own paper for Sophia's class on representations of adolescence in young adult literature, a challenging topic even for university students. She gestured to Sophia to
come closer to whisper something in her ear: "The high school students know this
stuff better than *we* do!"

   Through this culminating assessment, a presentation of their learning about
adolescence to a university audience, the nine high school seniors demonstrated
their new understandings by *teaching* future and current teachers novel ideas about
adolescence. The youth were teaching the "adults."

Assessment *and* Advocacy

In this chapter, we argue that adopting a sociocultural view of adolescence as an
approach to adolescent literacy opens up unique opportunities for shaping assessments that embed advocacy within them. Because the general approach we

promote—focusing on representations of adolescence through a sociocultural perspective in English class—presents nondominant views of youth that counter many
established beliefs about adolescence, when teachers explicitly teach youth these
ideas, students become uniquely positioned as knowledgeable about information
and perspectives unknown to many around them. By positioning youth as knowledgeable, especially about the topic of adolescence, and even more so in relation
to other youth or adults who likely do not know this information, assessments that
focus on new ideas of adolescence can be seen as inherently part of advocacy efforts
to promote social change.

Therefore, teachers have the opportunity to craft assessments that invite
students to share their emerging ideas about adolescents/ce and texts through print
and digital writing, public speaking, and other forms of expression to a range of
audiences as a means of civic engagement or advocacy. In other words, if teachers
take up cultural views of adolescence as a construct and teach those views explicitly
to their students, then one way that teachers can ascertain the degree to which students genuinely understand this new knowledge is to design assessments wherein
their students propagate these views in a range of public spaces.

As an example of what we are proposing, in Chapter 3, Bethany's students
created media texts to disseminate throughout their school that critiqued or revised
negative portrayals of youth to help stimulate other students' thinking about
these ideas and depictions. Additionally, Rachel's students, whom we discussed in
Chapter 2 and whom we previewed in this chapter's opening, knew that their units
would end with an assessment requiring them to synthesize and present their learning to a live audience of teacher candidates and university faculty in an effort to
demonstrate the effects of understanding this complex way of re-thinking adolescence. Both the students presenting and the teacher candidates in the audience—
many of whom were studying the same texts as the high school students—found
the dialogue stimulating and energizing for their work in schools.

Though each of these assessments differs in its specific focus and purpose,
they both share at least two features. First, youth are positioned as knowledgeable
about a topic that most adults and other youth know little about. In this positioning alone, teachers participate in reshaping conceptions and realities tied to
adolescence through English curriculum design. Second, by positioning youth to
engage with ideas in public spaces in these ways, students participate in the world,
in their communities, in their schools and classrooms as social activists, advocates
promoting social change around issues that matter deeply to them. Extending the
examples already offered in preceding sections of the book, this chapter presents
additional ideas for how teachers might re-think their assessments to embed such
advocacy in relation to real audiences when they elect to re-think adolescence as
part of their English language arts curriculum.

To be clear, teachers interested in engaging their students in critiques of adolescence do not have to assess their students' learning through public advocacy projects. Teachers have myriad options for assessing such learning. For example, you will remember that Rachel's AP English students, discussed in Chapter 2, wrote traditional practice essay exams as one culminating assessment that complemented their public talks to Sophia's university audience. However, what we wish to highlight in this chapter is that since the *content* of adolescence as a cultural construct is itself likely new to most audiences your students might encounter, teachers have a unique opportunity to create ways for students to present their learning to others. And in so doing, students will be automatically engaged in social change and advocacy. If teachers are (understandably) concerned about how such projects might take up too much time or other resources, the school itself and even the classroom and its extensions into online arenas could function as apt public spaces for such efforts.

In the remainder of this chapter, we will help you think further about the exciting prospect of shaping assessments that are authentic, challenging for students, and focused on a topic that your students are likely to be very excited about: adolescence. In addition, the assessments will be positioning your students as authorities on what they are writing and creating and doing.

To begin, we'll offer some background on why this approach to assessment makes sense by discussing some research that supports our suggestions, much of which you likely already know about (e.g., the need for authentic assessment). Then, we will share a host of idea kernels to consider for shaping assessments tied to adolescence in your curriculum. Many of these ideas came directly out of the chapters that preceded this one; others are ideas that we have either seen enacted or would love to see teachers try out.

Research and Theory

For teachers engaging in effective assessment practices, you already know that one well-established idea in education about how to make assessment work well is to make it "authentic": Do your best to make students' major projects focus on an audience that exceeds the teacher, and that is appropriate to the task you have asked them to complete (Wiggins & McTighe, 2005, pp. 153–54). Especially for teachers who have worked with the National Writing Project or a more regional Writing Project organization, this message of making a writing assessment "authentic" by ensuring that student writers have an audience beyond that of the teacher is likely familiar. In previous work with a high school English teacher, for example, Rob had great success in creating a tenth-grade curriculum whereby the students had to develop and disseminate research texts for "real" audiences. This added dimension to what was an otherwise ordinary assessment facilitated a much deeper engagement with the research and writing process. (See Borsheim & Petrone [2006] for more on this unit of study.)

In addition, drawing on ideas about assessment and curriculum design from Wiggins and McTighe's "backwards design" approach in their well-known book, *Understanding by Design* (2005), another key feature of effective assessment is that it is designed around *problems* rather than mere *exercises*. As the authors explain it, when teachers design assessments that are mere "exercises," they tend to be "school-based" assessments that are cleaned up, discrete, predetermined, and sometimes have "right answers." In contrast, "problem-based" assessments ask students to apply the knowledge and skills they have learned in order to find solutions, thereby demonstrating their ability to perform the content. For this reason, authentic, problem-based assessments are messy, involve lots of steps, require students to use their judgment, and justify their solutions. (For more on this distinction, see Wiggins & McTighe's [2005] chapter "Thinking Like an Assessor.")

To complement these ideas about assessment in general, in our own field of English education, Ernest Morrell (2005) has challenged English teachers to engage in a "critical English education." He defines a critical English education through three key features. First, it focuses on how language conveys meanings that can either promote or disrupt the status quo of power relations between people. Second, a critical English education teaches youth the skills needed to analyze dominant texts as well as to write their own texts that speak back to those dominant texts toward social justice goals. Finally, Morrell encourages teachers to utilize youths' everyday language practices to connect them to more academic literacies. Morrell writes about the importance of using specific kinds of curricula that position youth—especially traditionally disenfranchised youth, such as Rachel's students from Chapter 2, as well as their teachers—as social activists through literacy practices learned in English class. In this article, Morrell asks, "How seriously do we take our beliefs about the role of literacy education in promoting individual and social transformations?" (2005, p. 319).

By taking these ideas together—(1) the need for authentic assessments for students, (2) the importance of designing culminating projects that are problem-based rather than mere exercises, and (3) the value of designing curriculum that draws on youths' existing knowledge to move them toward literacy practices that engage them in social justice activism—we see a perfect recipe for English assessments focused on adolescence. Because critical views of adolescence are nondominant, and because youth themselves stand to benefit from engaging critically with a range of dominant texts that portray youth in demeaning and diminishing ways, shaping projects that invite youth to engage with these ideas through texts that share these ideas with others automatically engages youth and you in a critical

English education. Additionally, by shaping projects that involve youth promoting these ideas beyond English class and their teacher as the audience, the assessments will be authentic. Finally, because the purpose of the projects potentially involves affecting social change by attempting to educate others and even change others' minds about ideas tied to adolescence, the process of figuring out how to do this effectively is a "problem-based" process rather than one that feels like a school-based "exercise."

In the next section, we offer some sketches of ideas that you might like to think about and try out as is or modify to better fit your curriculum, communities, and students. Many of the ideas build from the content we have shared in prior chapters (e.g., "confident characterizations" of adolescence discussed especially in Chapters 1 and 4).

Assessment Possibilities

As we discuss several possibilities for how re-thinking adolescence helps to re-think assessment, an overarching concept that runs throughout all of these ideas is an emphasis on re-positioning youth as *contributors* to and *producers* of knowledge. We find it quite ironic that within education there are all sorts of spaces where adults (e.g., teachers, parents, administrators, politicians, policymakers) talk *about* youth and make decisions on their behalf but less frequently talk *with* youth to consult with them about their learning and invest them more in the process. Therefore, we highlight assessment possibilities that privilege students creating texts, delivering presentations, and otherwise engaging with advocacy and social justice goals through literacy and the English language arts.

Interview/Research Projects

- As an expository writing opportunity, ask students to take one of the "confident characterizations" (e.g., age, hormones, slow coming of age, peer-orientation) or common stereotypes of adolescence to investigate and write about. This research can be done, for instance, by having students interview and study specific youth. Does the confident characterization or stereotype hold? If not, what does your research show you about what determines what a fifteen-year-old is like, or whether youth in your school or life outside school succumb to peer pressure out of a drive for peer-orientedness? Students can also examine how these stereotypes show up in media, the public, and popular culture as well as in the literature they read. How are these stereotypes made to seem natural or normal? If they are critiqued, how are they examined?

- Research your school and community to see what assumptions and ideas of adolescence are operating within them. How does the school and/or community define, talk about, and/or label youth? Students can note and analyze the various posters, for example, hanging in the school and community that position youth in particular ways. Students can analyze teachers' talk about students to see what embedded assumptions about youth circulate in it and inform pedagogy. Perhaps students can even interview teachers and administrators to get their perspectives on youth.

- Examine school policies for the reasoning relied on as they pertain to youth. School dress codes are particularly generative for this activity as these often suggest important underlying messages about issues of "appropriateness" tied with age, gender, and adolescence. To start, students can do a textual analysis of the school policy related to the issue (e.g., dress code): What does the policy say and what is the rationale for the rule? From there, students can interview teachers, students, community members, and administrators to get their perspectives on the policy. Perhaps the students can even compare their school policy to other schools' policies. Secondary research can be done on recent instances reported in the media of students violating school dress code policies. The project can culminate in an analysis of school policies, particularly for their linkages to ideas of youth, with student recommendations or commentaries about the existing rules and possible changes to them.

- Investigate books banned within the school, community, or in neighboring communities. So often books banned in schools say more about an institution's or culture's conception of youth than about the literary texts themselves. As with the school policy analysis project outlined above, students can first identify which books have been challenged and/or banned and then interview librarians and media specialists, in addition to other school personnel, about how they understand the reasoning for the censorship. Students could then mull over their own positions about the book challenge(s) or banning(s), offering their analysis based on perceptions of youth, and, perhaps, advocating for the accessibility of particular texts to administration, librarians, and local school councils. (To read more about this possibility, see Alyssa Niccolini's 2015 article, "Precocious Knowledge: Using Banned Books to Engage in a Youth Lens.")

- Provide extracurricular opportunities for students to extend in-class projects. For example, students could write an editorial for the school newspaper on how stereotypes of adolescence affect their schooling life, or they could craft a longer journalistic exposé on how youth are constructed through practice and policy in school and society. Similarly, students could write for local media outlets (e.g., www.patch.com) in order to share their ideas on the social outcomes of "confident characterizations" of adolescence with a wider audience. Might there even be a way to work with these ideas within the school yearbook? Or might teachers work on creating a special event at the school or in the community to raise awareness of these critical issues?

Creative Writing Projects

- Take one of the "confident characterizations" of adolescence (e.g., age, hormones, slow coming of age, peer-orientation) and craft a short piece of fiction that challenges that trait. You might challenge the trait explicitly, like Sáenz in *Aristotle and Dante Discover the Secrets of the Universe* when he has Ari make fun of the idea that fifteen-year-olds don't yet qualify as people. If you try this approach, what facet of conventional adolescence will you challenge? Alternately, you could omit age references altogether, like Block does in *Weetzie Bat*. If you try the latter, what common expectations tied to youth might you challenge through your portrayal? (See Chapter 4 for a fuller treatment of these ideas as they are depicted in these young adult novels.)

- Similar to the previous possibility, students can satirize common conceptions of adolescence through fiction, poetry, or even digital texts, including through creating a short film. They can select a particular stereotype or try to work several into their text. For example, while teaching *The Catcher in the Rye* one year, Rob had his students create a satirical advertisement for Pencey Prep drawing on Holden's critiques of the school's conceptions of youth. In addition to the concepts of adolescence, an assessment like this can also work well to facilitate students' understanding of the elements of satire (and fiction or poetry as well). Alternatively, students could write satirical "non–young adult fiction" that features youth. How might adult characters in such a text be portrayed? Youth in relation to them? A satirical YA text like *Feed* (2002), or even a book like *The Hunger Games* (2008), could provide an entry point for thinking of ways texts can satirize normative conceptions of youth—and adulthood.

- Students could also craft creative nonfiction pieces, such as personal memoirs or anecdotes (in the vein of David Sedaris or Joan Didion or Annie Dillard), that use their own lives as stories of an alternative adolescence. Through their own stories, they could present how youth break the stereotypes that are so often presented in Hollywood depictions—such as "teen" movies like *Project X* and the *Bring It On* franchise—or local media reports that use isolated events to decry the "waywardness" of youth.

- Students can engage in "online fandom" or "transmedia," discussed by Antero Garcia and Marcelle Haddix in their 2015 article, "Reading YA with 'Dark Brown Skin.'" In this article, the authors discuss the possibilities of inviting students to engage in existing "participatory culture" online around YA texts wherein fans develop and continue storylines begun by their original authors and now taken over by fans. In doing so, however, Garcia and Haddix warn that such efforts may perpetuate rather than interrogate and critique problematic views of race and gender. How might you take their suggestions about inviting students to engage in "transmedia" around YAL but now focus it on representations of adolescence that your students could comment on?

Visual and Media Projects

- As referenced in Chapter 3, students can interrogate the various ways youth are discussed and depicted in the media. Through this exploration, students will be poised to create (and hopefully disseminate) media texts, such as their own YouTube channels or blogs, that critique common, negative depictions of youth and offer revised, more positive representations of youth. In this way, students would be re-branding adolescence visually through an advertising campaign of sorts that shows young people in ways that defy stereotypes. What kinds of images would you utilize? What kinds of captions would help to address your points about adolescence?

- Check out images of youth on sites that house photographs or drawings available for purchase by publications (e.g., Thinkstock, iStock) by looking for images of "adolescence." What do you notice about these images? What comes up when you look for "adolescence" in "stocks" of images about youth? Now, craft your own image-based site for "adolescence" by engaging in a photograph and drawing project that represents youth outside of "stock" images: What will you photograph or draw? What might you write as an "artist's statement" to explain your artwork to a local news reporter who might want—or should want—to know about your project?

- Create (political) cartoons about adolescence. In the style of the *New Yorker* cartoon that we referenced in Chapter 1, the one with the caption that showed parents grounding an adolescent until his cerebral cortex matured, visualize a cartoon campaign that revises—via comical critique—views of adolescence and youth. What are some stock ideas and images of youth that students could critique? What are some jokes—some plays with words—that students could craft to comment on conventional and problematic views of adolescence?

- Investigate the ways youth are (and are not) discussed in politics and by politicians. Have students follow national political campaigns and local politics for politicians' views of youth. How are youth talked about (if at all) by politicians? Have students examine newspapers and other media outlets for news coverage of youth. What types of stories are told about youth in these news outlets? What narratives and representations of youth are missing? From these explorations, have students create texts to counter the mis- and/ or under-representations and disseminate them to the politicians and news outlets they investigate.

Public Speaking Projects

- Take the idea discussed in the opening vignette at the beginning of this chapter and in Chapter 2 about the high school students discussing their learning about adolescence to a university audience and think about ways you can establish connections with your local university to facilitate similar types of experiences for your students. Are there possibilities, for instance, whereby high school students could put together workshops to deliver to future high school teachers?

- Similarly, you could actively promote your students by finding events or spaces in which they could present or perform their understandings about adolescence. For example, as part of a year-long event series celebrating the history of Latinx Americans in Baltimore, Mark hosted a panel on the evolving relationships between the African American and Latinx communities in the city. He invited high school students to sit alongside professors, community activists, and teachers to ensure that youth had a voice in the conversation. The presence of youth at such events could be used as a productive way to disrupt stereotypical notions of adolescence.

- Outside of university-based teacher education, consider where and how else your students might take their learning about adolescence as a cultural construct to a public audience. For example, is there a possibility of setting up a half-day, community TEDx series you could help students coordinate so they could educate and dialogue with people about the ways youth are positioned in the local community?

- Invite students to put together and deliver a presentation at a professional conference related to their participation in the work around reconceptualizing adolescence. Perhaps even invite them to write with you for professional publications—something like an article for *English Journal* or *Voices from the Middle*.

- Create opportunities for students to be guest speakers in other classes—in your school, in another high school, or even middle and elementary schools. What if they visited the closest middle school (if they are high school students) or fifth-grade class (if they are middle school students) and shared their learning about adolescence? How would they change their presentation—including tone, voice, and diction—for that audience than for one focused on peers, or different adults?

- Students can conduct a needs assessment for their local community and then create texts to disseminate in order to initiate change. The process would involve determining a social issue related to youth that is not being met by local policies and practices—e.g., perhaps the local government recently cut funds for community centers—and then determining solutions for that issue. In one project, Rob worked with a group of high school students to investigate the possibility of a music venue in their community for local bands to play. The students could research questions such as: What resources are and are not readily available for youth? Who determines these? How can youth engage in the political process in order to advocate for their needs within the community? Perhaps, based on their research, they can give a presentation at a town hall or school board meeting, write letters to the editor, or otherwise engage adults in positions of power to help effect change in the community to better meet the needs of youth.

Closing Thoughts

This book has taken the premises behind the helpful NCTE policy brief on adolescent literacy and exposed the ways that adding a new consideration—one focused on a sociocultural view of adolescence—would make the brief even more robust and invest English language arts teaching with a new, much-needed analytic and productive dimension. By sharing our own learning and research on the ways ideas about adolescence have changed our teaching and the instruction of teachers with whom we have had the privilege to work, we hope to introduce you to a range of practices and additional resources for taking up what we see as an important social justice stance and perspective in your own middle and high school classrooms. To continue your thinking about the ideas we have shared in this book, the annotated bibliography that follows highlights some key articles and books that have informed our own ideas about youth and the social category of adolescence, and/or showcase additional ways that folks in our field have applied a critical view of adolescence to English language arts teaching. We hope you find these texts as informing and transformative of your practices as we have.

Annotated Bibliography

Kokkola, Lydia.
Fictions of Adolescent Carnality: Sexy Sinners and Delinquent Deviants.
Amsterdam; Philadelphia: John Benjamins. 2013.

For any teacher interested in understanding the many restrictions on sexual depictions in texts that might be used in school, Kokkola's book offers both a theoretical explanation and many examples of how sexuality is depicted in young adult literature. Her explanation of societal problems with adolescent sexuality is a sociocultural one, like the explanation we rely on, but she focuses on the role of sex and innocence in conceptions of childhood and adolescence. Then she reviews scores of Anglophone young adult literature since the 1960s to show how conservative they are in depictions of sexual youth.

Lewis, Mark A.
"Illustrating Youth: A Critical Examination of the Artful Depictions of Adolescent Characters in Comics."
In Crag Hill, ed., *Teaching Comics through Multiple Lenses: Critical Perspectives* (pp. 49–61). New York: Routledge, 2016.

Lewis, Mark A., and E. Sybil Durand.
"Sexuality as Risk and Resistance in Young Adult Literature."
In Crag Hill, ed., *The Critical Merits of Young Adult Literature: Coming of Age* (pp. 38–54). New York: Routledge, 2014.

These two chapters provide Youth Lens analyses of young adult literature similar to the ones we present in Chapter 4. "Sexuality as Risk and Resistance" focuses on how adolescents who engage in sexual thought and action are represented, particularly through risk and resistance formulations. In risk formulations, adolescent characters are punished—including through sickness and death of lovers, exile from their families, and incarceration—which sends the message to young readers that engaging in sexual thought and action will lead to negative, if not catastrophic, consequences. In resistance formulations, however, adolescent characters demonstrate conscious and confident understandings of their sexuality, thereby disrupting often stereotypical views of hormone-driven and out-of-control youth. "Illustrating Youth" examines how the choices of artists of young adult graphica reveal certain assumptions about adolescents and the "typical" adolescent experience. These depictions are based upon nostalgia, fabrication, and enchantment—which can interfere with attempts to present authentic and diverse lives of youth. For example, some artists relied upon certain scenes of high school life—such as the first day of school and homecoming parties—to spark nostalgic and enchanting memories to both celebrate and criticize the decisions of youth.

Petrone, Robert, Sophia Tatiana Sarigianides, and Mark A. Lewis.
"The 'Youth Lens': Analyzing Adolescence/ts in Literary Texts."
Journal of Literacy Research 46.4 (2014): 506–33.

This article introduces the Youth Lens to an English education audience. It explains that the idea of adolescence as a construct has been established by scholars in many fields for over a decade, but that the idea is barely making a ripple in teacher preparation programs and teaching. As the authors, we then make the case for the importance of centralizing revised conceptions of youth in our field of English teaching and show how this might look by introducing a critical lens for reading literature, especially young adult literature. We describe the lens, offer a heuristic for trying it out, and apply it to a fresh interpretation of *The*

Hunger Games by focusing on the role of setting in shaping whether Katniss is depicted as an "adult" or an "adolescent."

Sarigianides, Sophia Tatiana
"Rampant Teen Sex: Teen Sexuality and the Promise of Happiness as Obstacles to Rethinking Adolescence."
Journal of Youth Studies 17.8 (2014): 1061–76.

This article takes a scholarly look at how experienced teachers' resistance to revised ideas of adolescence are often due to a reluctance to think about young people as sexual. In other words, teachers who are interested in constructed views of adolescence get stuck once they realize that part of such revised views of youth involves understanding that youth are sexual. In their explanations of this as a problem, teachers reveal a worry that if they seem to "approve" of teen sex, they will be ruining young people's chances at (an adult) happiness "promised" to them by following the "right path" to adulthood.

Sarigianides, Sophia Tatiana, Mark A. Lewis, and Robert Petrone, eds.
"Re-thinking 'Adolescence' to Re-imagine English [Special issue]."
English Journal 104.3 (2015).

This special-themed issue of *English Journal* is a collection of practitioner-focused articles that illustrate a range of ways the ideas presented throughout this book can be applied to secondary teaching situations. The articles are relatively short, engaging, and practical, and they explore the following topics:

- Censorship and book banning;
- Teaching pop culture through a youth lens;
- Disrupting dominant visions of youth of color;
- How youth use social media for social justice;
- Analyzing first person narration of young adult literature;

- Re-thinking labels such as "struggling" readers;
- Media literacy to examine conceptions of youth;
- Re-positioning youth as cosmopolitan intellectuals.

Perhaps more than any other text beyond this book, we suggest this special-themed issue as the apposite entry into the work of how re-thinking adolescence as a cultural construct can help re-shape teaching the English language arts.

Sieben, Nicole
"*Openly Straight*: A Look at Teaching LGBTQ Young Adult Sports Literature through a Queer Theory Youth Lens."
In Darla Linville and David Lee Carlson, eds., *Beyond Borders: Queer Eros and Ethos (Ethics) in LGBTQ Young Adult Literature* (pp. 199–217). New York: Peter Lang, 2015.

As a complement to the curricula we present in Chapters 2 through 4, Sieben expertly provides another way for incorporating a sociocultural understanding of adolescence/ts within the English language arts classroom. Sieben layers on queer theory to a Youth Lens analysis to demonstrate how teachers can facilitate classroom discussions on both normed conceptions of adolescence, and gender and sexuality. She focuses on young adult sports literature due to the barriers many LGBTQ youth face when participating in organized sports, including (not) fitting into student-athlete stereotypes and homophobic slurs from both teammates and opponents. After outlining her complex, multifaceted theoretical framework of a queer theory Youth Lens, Sieben provides a possible curriculum for Konigsberg's *Openly Straight* (2013) for teachers who want to support secondary students in questioning social norms. For example, these activities ask students to consider how setting can influence adolescent identities, and how a queer reading of sports interactions can reveal a complicated metaphor for adolescent life.

Thein, Amanda Haertling, Mark A. Sulzer, and Renita Schmidt.

"Evaluating the Democratic Merit of Young Adult Literature: Lessons from Two Versions of Wes Moore's Memoir."
English Journal 103.2 (2013): 52–59.

For us, this article offers one of the clearest illustrations of how many young adult texts rely on dominant ideas of adolescence to teach particular lessons to and about youth. If you are struggling a bit with the ideas from Chapter 4 or want another illustration of the ideas in it, this article would be a great read. In essence, the authors discuss two versions of a memoir—one marketed for adults and another revised for young adults—and find significant differences between these. They explain how the youth adaptation reduces the complexities of the book's critique of how societal and institutional forces influence people's lives and instead positions the situations in the book as being primarily about individual choice. The authors of the article demonstrate how these changes in the adaptation rely upon assumptions of youth grounded in developmental psychology that reduce social and cultural influences on youths' lives, and as a result emphasize lessons in "good decision making."

Vadeboncoeur, Jennifer Andrea, and Lisa Patel Stevens, eds.

Re/constructing "the Adolescent": Sign, Symbol, and Body.
New York: Peter Lang, 2005.

For the three of us, this book proved pivotal in both our understandings of adolescence as a cultural construct and how dominant ideas of youth shape our development of teaching practices. Though many of the chapters are excellent, we suggest especially Chapter 1 ("Naturalised, Restricted, Packaged, and Sold: Reifying the Fictions of 'Adolescent' and 'Adolescence'") and Chapter 5 ("'Gotta Be Worse': Literacy, Schooling, and Adolescent Youth Offenders"). Chapter 1 explains how many current ideas of youth are "fictions" rather than verifiable "truth." Specifically, the chapter explores facets of the history of adolescence, as well as how language and the media help to create and naturalize ideas of youth. Chapter 5 explains how, in a class in an alternative high school, dominant ideas of youth created a set of expectations for both the students and the teachers whereby they interacted with each other in limiting ways based on these expectations. In this way, concepts of adolescence constrained how teachers thought of students and even how students thought of themselves.

References

Abraham, M., Bendinger, J., Bernstein, A., Bliss, T. A., Cullen, P., Scanlon, C. . . . Wong, M. (Producers), & Reed, P. (Director). (2000). *Bring it on* [Motion picture]. United States: Universal Pictures.

Adichie, C. N. (2009, July). *The danger of the single story* [Video file]. Retrieved from http://www.ted.com/talks/chimamanda_adichie_the_danger_of_a_single_story.html

Adler, M., & Rougle, E. (2005). *Building literacy through classroom discussion: Research-based strategies for developing critical readers and thoughtful writers in middle school.* New York: Scholastic.

Alexie, S. (2007). *The absolutely true diary of a part-time Indian.* New York: Little, Brown and Company.

Allen, A. (2014, September 1). Risky behavior by teens can be explained in part by how their brains change. *The Washington Post.* Retrieved from https://www.washingtonpost.com/national/health-science/risky-behavior-by-teens-can-be-explained-in-part-by-how-their-brains-change/2014/08/29/28405df0-27d2-11e4-8593-da634b334390_story.html

Alvermann, D. E. (2009). Sociocultural constructions of adolescence and young people's literacies. In L. Christenbury, R. Bomer, & P. Smagorinsky (Eds.), *Handbook of Adolescent Literacy Research* (pp. 14–28). New York: Guilford Press.

Alvermann, D. E., & Hinchman, K. A. (Eds.). (2012). *Reconceptualizing the literacies in adolescents' lives: Bridging the everyday/academic divide* (3rd ed.). New York: Routledge.

Anderson, M. T. (2002). *Feed.* Cambridge, MA: Candlewick Press.

Appleman, D. (2015). *Critical encounters in secondary English: Teaching literary theory to adolescents* (3rd ed.). New York: Teachers College Press.

Belle and Sebastian. (1996). Me and the Major. On *If You're Feeling Sinister* [CD]. New York: Matador Records.

Block, F. L. (1989). *Weetzie bat.* New York: Harper-Collins.

Borsheim, C., & Petrone, R. (2006). Teaching the research paper for local action. *English Journal, 95*(4), 78–83.

Borsheim-Black, C. (2015). Reading pop culture and young adult literature though the youth lens. *English Journal, 104*(3), 29–34.

Bruce, D. (2015). Re-constructing and re-presenting teenagers: Using media literacy to examine cultural constructions of adolescents. *English Journal, 104*(3), 68–74.

Budnick, S., Ewing, M. P., Heineman, A., Phillips, T., Richards, S., Rona, A., Silver, J. (Producers), & Nourizadeh, N. (Director). (2012). *Project X* [Motion picture]. United States: Warner Bros.

Chbosky, S. (1999). *The perks of being a wallflower.* New York: MTV Books/Gallery Books.

College Board. (2008). *AP English Literature and Composition 2008 Free Response Questions.*

Collins, S. (2008). *The hunger games.* New York: Scholastic Press.

DeJaynes, T., & Curmi, C. (2015). Youth as cosmopolitan intellectuals. *English Journal, 104*(3), 75–80.

Dretzin, R. (Writer), & Goodman, B. (Director). (2001). The merchants of cool [Television series episode]. In D. Fanning, & M. Sullivan. *Frontline.* New York: PBS Home Video.

Falter, M. M. (2016). Addressing assumptions about adolescents in a preservice YAL course. *The ALAN Review, 43*(2), 51–61.

Finders, M. (1999). Raging hormones: Stories of adolescence and implications for teacher preparation. *Journal of Adolescent and Adult Literacy, 42*(4), 252–63.

Finders, M. J. (2005). "Gotta be worse": Literacy, schooling, and adolescent youth offenders. In J. A. Vadeboncoeur & L. P. Stevens (Eds.), *Re/constructing "the adolescent": Sign, symbol, and body* (pp. 97–122). New York: Peter Lang.

Free, C. (2016, June 8). Montana teen stages protest after school demands she wear bra: "I was told a male teacher had complained he was uncomfortable." *People*. Retrieved from http://people.com/celebrity/montana-teen-stages-protest-after-school-demands-she-wear-bra/

Garcia, A., & Haddix, M. (2015). Reading YA with "dark brown skin": Race, community, and Rue's uprising. *The ALAN Review, 42*(2), 37–44.

Green, J. (2005). *Looking for Alaska*. New York: Speak.

Groenke, S., Haddix, M., Glenn, W., Kirkland, D., Price-Dennis, D. & Coleman-King, C. (2015). Disrupting and dismantling the dominant vision of youth of color. *English Journal, 104*(3), 35–40.

Hall, G. S. (1904). *Adolescence: Its psychology and its relation to psychology, anthropology, sociology, sex, crime, religion, and education*. New York: D. Appleton.

Herz, S. K., & Gallo, D. R. (2005). *From Hinton to Hamlet: Building bridges between young adult literature and the classics* (2nd ed.). Westport, CT: Greenwood.

Jay-Z. (2009). Young forever. On *The Blueprint 3* [CD]. New York: Roc Nation.

Katz, J., Earp, J. (Screenwriters), & Jhally, S. (Director). (2002). *Tough guise: Violence, media, and the crisis in masculinity* (Motion Picture or DVD). Northampton, MA: Media Education Foundation.

Kellner, D., & Share, J. (2005). Toward critical media literacy: Core concepts, debates, organizations, and policy. *Discourse: Studies in the Cultural Politics of Education, 26*(3), 369–86. doi: 10.1080/01596300500200169

Kincaid, J. (1978, June 26) Girl. *The New Yorker*. Retrieved from http://www.newyorker.com/magazine/1978/06/26/girl

Kirkland, D. E. (2008). "The rose that grew from concrete": Postmodern blackness and new English education. *English Journal, 97*(5), 69–75.

Kist, W., Srsen, K., & Bishop, B. F. (2015). Social media and "kids today": A counter-narrative from a US high school. *English Journal, 104*(3), 41–46.

Lesko, N. (2012). *Act your age! A cultural construction of adolescence* (2nd ed.). New York: Routledge.

Lewis, M. A., & Petrone, R. (2010). "Although adolescence need not be violent . . .": Preservice teachers' connections between "adolescence" and literacy curriculum. *Journal of Adolescent & Adult Literacy, 53*(5), 398–407. doi: 10.1598/JAAL.53.5.5

Lewis, M. A., Petrone, R., & Sarigianides, S. T. (2016). Acting adolescent? Critical examinations of the youth-adult binary in *Feed* and *Looking for Alaska*. *The ALAN Review, 43*(2), 43–50.

Morrell, E. (2004). *Linking literacy and popular culture: Finding connections for lifelong learning*. Norwood, MA: Christopher-Gordon.

Morrell, E. (2005). Critical English education. *English Education, 37*(4), 312–21.

Morrell, E., Deuñas, R., Garcia, V., & López, J. (2013). *Critical media pedagogy: Teaching for achievement in city schools*. New York: Teachers College Press.

Moshman, D. (2011, May 17). The teenage brain: Debunking the 5 biggest myths. *The Huffington Post*. Retrieved from http://www.huffingtonpost.com/david-moshman/adolescents-and-their-tee_b_858360.html

Myers, W. D. (1999). *Monster*. New York: HarperCollins.

Myers, W. D. (2014, March 15). Where are the people of color in children's books? *The New York Times*. Retrieved from https://www.nytimes.com/2014/03/16/opinion/sunday/where-are-the-people-of-color-in-childrens-books.html

National Council of Teachers of English. (2007). *Adolescent literacy: A policy research brief*. Retrieved from http://www.ncte.org/library/NCTEFiles/Resources/Positions/Chron0907ResearchBrief.pdf

Niccolini, A. D. (2015). Precocious knowledge: Using banned books to engage in a youth lens. *English Journal, 104*(3), 22–28.

Perry, K., McKee, B., Luke, Dr., Martin, M. (2011). Last Friday night (T.G.I.F.) [CD]. [Katy Perry]. On *Teenage Dream*. Los Angeles: Capitol Records.

Petrone, R., & Borsheim, C. (2008). "It just seems to be more intelligent": Critical literacy in high school English. In L. Wallowitz (Ed.), *Critical literacy as resistance: Teaching for social justice across the secondary curriculum* (pp. 179–206). New York: Peter Lang.

Petrone, R., & Lewis, M. A. (2012). Deficits, therapists, and a desire to distance: Secondary English pre-service teachers' reasoning about their future students. *English Education, 44*(3), 254–87.

Petrone, R., Sarigianides, S. T., & Lewis, M. A. (2014). The "youth lens": Analyzing adolescence/ts in literary texts. *Journal of Literacy Research, 46*(4), 506–33.

Sáenz, B. A. (2012). *Aristotle and Dante discover the secrets of the universe.* New York: Simon & Schuster.

Salinger, J. D. (1951/1991). *The catcher in the rye.* Boston: Little, Brown.

Sarigianides, S. T. (2012). Tensions in teaching adolescence/ts: Analyzing resistances in a young adult literature course. *Journal of Adolescent & Adult Literacy, 56*(3), 222–30.

Sarigianides, S. T. (2014). Rampant teen sex: Teen sexuality and the promise of happiness as obstacles to re-thinking adolescence. *Journal of Youth Studies, 17*(8), 1061–76.

Sarigianides, S. T., Lewis, M. A., & Petrone, R. (2015). How re-thinking adolescence helps re-imagine the teaching of English. *English Journal, 104*(3), 13–18.

Schor, J. (2005). *Born to buy: The commercialized child and the new consumer culture.* New York: Scribner.

Smith, M. W., & Wilhelm, J. D. (2010). *Fresh takes on teaching literary elements: How to teach what really matters about character, setting, point of view, and theme.* New York & Urbana, IL: Scholastic & NCTE.

Sulzer, M., & Thein, A. H. (2016). Reconsidering the hypothetical adolescent in evaluating and teaching young adult literature. *Journal of Adolescent & Adult Literacy, 60*(2), 163–71.

Thein, A. H., Sulzer, M., & Schmidt, R. (2013). Evaluating the democratic merit of young adult literature: Lessons from two versions of Wes Moore's memoir. *English Journal, 103*(2), 52–59.

Thein, A. H., & Sulzer, M. A. (2015). Illuminating discourses of youth through the study of first-person narration in young adult literature. *English Journal, 104*(3), 47–53.

Tosh, P. (1968). Can't blame the youth. On *Honorary Citizen* [CD]. JAD Record Company.

Underwood, W. (1987). The body biography: A framework for student writing. *English Journal, 76*(8), 44–48.

Waller, A. (2010). *Constructing adolescence in fantastic realism.* New York: Routledge.

Wiggins, G. P., & McTighe, J. (2005). *Understanding by design* (2nd ed.). Alexandria, VA: Association for Supervision and Curriculum Development.

Index

Authors

Sophia Tatiana Sarigianides is associate professor of English education at Westfield State University in Western Massachusetts, where she coordinates the English education program. Prior to her work in teacher preparation, she taught middle and high school English in Southern California for ten years. Her research and publications focus on constructions of adolescence in teacher and youth thinking, and in representations of young adult literature. She also studies and writes about the role of race in teacher thinking, in white teacher identity, and in the teaching of English. She has published in *English Journal*, *The ALAN Review*, *Journal of Adolescent & Adult Literacy*, *Journal of Literacy Research*, *Journal of Youth Studies*, *Curriculum Inquiry*, and *Educational Theory*.

Robert Petrone is associate professor and director of English education at Montana State University. Prior to his role as English education faculty, he taught secondary reading and English in Colorado and New York. Unified by a social justice framework, his research includes reconceptualizing "adolescence/ts" in English education, the role of critical literacy and popular culture in secondary English classrooms, and learning and literacy in youth cultures. Most recently, he has begun research on English education in rural contexts. In addition to book chapters, his work has appeared in *Journal of Literacy Research*, *Teaching and Teacher Education*, *English Education*, *Journal of Adolescent & Adult Literacy*, *Journal of Language and Literacy Education*, *The ALAN Review*, and *English Journal*.

Mark A. Lewis is associate professor of literacy education at Loyola University Maryland, where he teaches courses in children's and young adult literature, content area literacy, and English methods. He also spent several years teaching English language arts and English as a second language in Arizona and Colorado. His research examines literary competence, conceptions of youth, and young adult literature. He also has begun work examining how secondary English language arts teachers support literacy development of emerging bilingual students. His work has appeared in *Journal of Literacy Research*, *English Education*, *Journal of Adolescent and Adult Literacy*, *Middle Grades Research Journal*, *The ALAN Review*, and *Teaching English Language Arts to English Language Learners* (2016).

This book was typeset in Janson Text and BotonBQ by
Barbara Frazier.

Typefaces used on the cover include American Typewriter,
Frutiger, and Formata.

The book was printed on 60-lb. White Offset paper
by Versa Press, Inc.

30% Total Recycled Fiber